PROFITABLE BRILLIANCE

HOW PROFESSIONAL SERVICES FIRMS
BECOME THOUGHT LEADERS

By Russ Alan Prince and Bruce H. Rogers

Forbes

FORBES MEDIA
60 FIFTH AVENUE
NEW YORK, NY 10011

This book is designed to provide accurate and authoritative information on
the subject matter covered. This publication is sold with the understanding
that neither the publisher nor the authors are engaged in rendering legal,
medical, accounting, financial or other professional service or advice in
specific situations. Although prepared by professionals, this publication
should not be utilized as a substitute for professional advice in specific
situations. If legal, medical, accounting, financial or other professional
advice is required the services of the appropriate professional should be
sought. Neither the authors nor the publisher may be held liable for any
misuse or misinterpretation of the information in this publication. All
information provided is believed and intended to be reliable, but accuracy
cannot be guaranteed by the authors or the publisher.

Cover design: Kevin Adkins

ISBN: 1475231369
ISBN-13: 9781475231366

DEDICATIONS

To Susan, Jessica & Sean for your support and inspiration.
— Bruce

To Sandi, Jerry & Ace—for making life great.
— Russ

INTRODUCTION

In 1993 the world's iconic computer company, IBM, almost went bankrupt and the company's CEO was forced to resign. So dismal were IBM's survival odds that no top-tier computer-industry CEO would take the job. IBM's board of directors, discouraged, put into place a plan to break IBM up into "Baby Blues" with the hope that shareholders would get at least something from the wreck.

At last IBM found a CEO, Louis Gerstner. An outsider from the financial services industry, Gerstner was able to discern IBM's true value underneath. IBM had the brand, he saw, it just had the wrong business model for the 1990s and beyond. So Gerstner did something that only an outsider could do. He declared that IBM would find its renaissance as an IT services company. When Gerstner retired in 1999 he was succeeded by Sam Palmisano, the executive who had built IBM into a global IT services juggernaut.

Today IBM is healthy. Its bet on professional services was the right one.

The demand for top-tier professional service firms has never been greater. It is being driven by these trends:

EXPONENTIAL TECHNOLOGIES

Today's driving technologies—computers, communication bandwidth, nanotechnology, digital manufacturing, artificial intelligence, engineered biological processes—all improve at exponential rates. But the human brain has evolved to think in linear terms. Thus a gap is growing between where the business world will be in two, five, ten and twenty years and where most business executives—who necessarily must focus on the 0-18 month timeframe—think it will be. Professional service firms that can guide clients safely to the future will do very well in the coming years.

BOOMING COMPETITION

As computer and communications technologies evolve toward free and infinite, barriers to entry in multiple businesses fall away. A decade ago, who could have imagined Amazon as the greatest potential threat to Walmart, or Skype and WiFi to AT&T and Verizon? What will tomorrow's 3D printing machines do to mass manufacturing and retail? What will self-diagnostic apps on your smart phone do the health care industry? Professional service firms that can help entrepreneurs and incumbents harness these new opportunities will be in high demand.

EXPANDING MARKETS

China's capitalistic revolution has produced a middle class of 300 million people in 30 years. Five billion people out of the world's seven billion now have cell phones. Two billion have web-enabled smart phones and that number is expected to triple by 2020. Facebook now has 700 million members. The market potential created by this new connected global middle class are salivating. But which professional service firms can help you exploit these developments?

Change and complexity will always be the professional service firm's best friends. What good news! The world is getting faster and more complex each day! The opportunity to build the next great marketing, advertising, public relations, accounting, legal and consulting firm is therefore ours to grab. But how? Authors

Russ Alan Prince and my Forbes colleague Bruce H. Rogers have studied professional firms for a quarter of a century. They apply their knowledge and wisdom—and most of all, foresight—in this brilliant book of tips and tactics.

Enjoy, learn and profit.

Rich Karlgaard
Forbes Publisher

FORWARD

The last twenty five years in the professional services industry has seen the rise of the "thought leader." Almost everyone, it seems, aspires to be a thought leader, and for good reason: Even in bad times, they are sought after by the most desirable clients. They have the greatest opportunity to put their mark on their field. And they have the easiest time attracting top talent to their organizations.

But if everyone wants to be a thought leader, there is little guidance on what thought leadership actually is, how it is achieved, and how it can be leveraged for the benefit of the firm. *Profitable Brilliance* seeks to provide that much-needed insight about this little-understood phenomenon.

Understanding thought leadership is important not just because of the benefits it brings, but because it goes to the very heart of our knowledge-intensive businesses. Ultimately, professional services is about helping people and organizations solve their problems and achieve their goals: An accountant might be helping a business owner with the strategic planning of his or her growing business. An architect might be designing a new house. But solving problems—even doing so successfully—actually raises another set of higher-level questions. What's the best way to solve the problem? How do you incorporate innovation in the solution? How will the problem present itself differently five years from now? We can even ask what we mean when we say that we've "solved a problem." The accountant might have helped develop a fine strategic plan with his or her client but has the plan been effectively executed? Have external factors changed making it necessary to adjust the plan?

These aren't just philosophical issues—they are central to what professional services is about. How we answer them defines the direction of the field, and how well we answer them determines how successfully we serve our clients. Thought leadership is about having meaningful answers to those higher-level questions, effectively communicating those answers to your market and leveraging the resulting reputation for the benefit of your firm.

My appreciation of the power of thought leadership came from my own experience. Like most people in professional services, I spend a fair amount of time at conferences, panel discussions and so on. And I realized that when the speaker presented material and data that went beyond the obvious and provided real insight with concrete conclusions or recommendations, I was always very interested and there was a lot of lively discussion, but if those things were lacking then I spent a lot of time looking at my watch.

Then I had a second realization, based on the feedback I was getting from clients: That I had a point of view worth sharing and should be making the effort to do so. This, of course, underscores an essential element of thought leadership—that it is not enough to have good ideas, but that those ideas must be effectively expressed. Unfortunately, I had never been very comfortable with public speaking. So I arranged for some training from a very good coach and got myself out there. I could have chosen not to do that—some people limit their thought leadership to writing. But there is no substitute for the direct interaction with one's audience and the opportunity it brings to refine your thinking. So even though I had to get a bit outside of my comfort zone, it was well worth it.

I've been fortunate in that my firm, Rothstein Kass, has always placed a high value on thought leadership. The firm believes that thought leadership, when done strategically and well, is an investment, not an expense. It also believes it is a process, which means that it can be monitored, improved and replicated. This approach allowed me to look at the success my colleague Rick Flynn, profiled in these pages. Rick has established himself as a thought leader in the family office arena with insightful, data-filled industry surveys. I adapted that strategy to my own area of private equity funds. And recently, we established a firm-wide Thought Leadership Committee to act as a driver for promoting best practices within the firm, sharing knowledge and setting priorities.

With client problems growing more complex, clients becoming more demanding, and competition between professional services firms more intense, the importance of thought leadership will only continue to increase. It pays to bear in mind that in addition to all the obvious benefits that come with being a thought leader—the larger market share, the greater authority and so on—there is another less obvious benefit that is perhaps even more compelling: it helps you become a better practitioner and be able to deliver greater value to your clients. The thought leadership process, when done deliberately, sharpens your ideas, leads you to new insights and focuses your message—benefits that provide success not just now, but in the future.

Thomas J. Angell
Principal
Rothstein Kass

TABLE OF CONTENTS

ABOUT THIS BOOK

For more than a quarter century we've been consulting with professional services firms, other corporate entities and individuals. One of the most intriguing and appealing areas we've focused on has been helping them become thought leaders. We've even been called in to assist a few of them to become celebrity thought leaders. In all these engagements, the financial benefits to these firms and individuals have been dramatic, and for many of them those benefits have been absolutely astounding.

Our ability to eruditely apply the array of principles, strategies, models and tactics that constitute the thought leadership process has been refined in the crucible of time, fired extensively by trial and error. Along the way, we've critically dissected our failures to correct errors and gained a better understanding of what works and why. We've also found powerful ways to accentuate our successes. In sum, we've had a lot of practice applying and subsequently refining the thought leadership process, with exceptional results.

Our professional backgrounds, coupled with a certain experience-based intellectual-organizational perspective, lend themselves to putting the puzzle pieces together. Our spot-on thought leadership products cut through the insidious clutter and solidly resonate with target audiences, usually resulting in a cadre of very loyal followers. This, in turn, with appropriate follow-up by the professional services firm, translates into appreciably greater revenues. It's this ability to connect the dots and make it all readily accessible that is the basis of our usefulness in helping professional services firms as well as individual professionals become thought leaders which, in turn, translates into exponentially greater success.

Because of the extensive benefits that accrue to thought leaders, especially when it comes to business development, there's a lot of high-powered buzz around what it takes to become one. Reality is much more humbling. There are often—although not always—minimal mental gymnastics required to create high-quality thought leadership products. All in all, it's predominantly a very systematic and straightforward endeavor where clever recurrently trumps smart. Significant success is not derived from an understanding of the thought leadership process per se, but from the adroit implementation of that process.

The thought leadership process is one that most any professional services firm, and even most any individual professional, can probably execute with great financial returns.

With the growing success of Forbes Insights, an ever-increasing number of managing partners at professional services firms have asked us about the nature and mechanics of the thought leadership process. Aside from wanting an overarching, clean and forthright understanding of the business logic behind being a thought leader, they were very interested in knowing the nature and operational aspects of the "machine" that produces thought leaders.

In this book, we explain the business logic of thought leadership as well as the machine's basic nature and operation. Our goal is to provide an overview of the motivations and means required to become a thought leader. We also address how a professional services firm can ratchet up its efforts, going beyond becoming a thought leader to becoming a celebrity thought leader. We describe all the major components of the thought leadership engine and explain how they fit together.

In dissecting the thought leadership process, we recognize that taking a broad-based approach—thereby making it applicable to potentially all manner of professional services firms as well as many other organizations—admittedly diminishes the richness of the process. It's not just that we're glossing over the nuances and particularities of the thought leadership process out of instructional necessity; we're pretending they don't even exist. This is a failing of this treatise that we recognize and apologize for in advance.

While our dissection of the thought leadership process is educational and informative, it's unfortunately only a skeleton. Although we're providing a powerful framework, the thought leadership process is only truly mastered experientially. We believe coupling a solid grasp of the fundamentals of the thought leadership process with experience is probably the optimal way to perfect the knowledge and skills required to consistently transition a professional services firm from a highly adept "unknown" to a highly adept "well respected and well known." Herein we're delivering the fundamentals.

INTERLUDE: MAGICIAN MAKES GOOD

GEOFF RAMSEY, CO-FOUNDER, EMARKETER

Geoff Ramsey is a man in motion. He exhibits boundless energy with an optimistic and confident outlook on life. As we sit down to dinner for this interview, he confesses that, not only is he training for a half-marathon, but that he is one of those lucky few people who has a higher than normal metabolism that allows him to eat anything and still remain rail thin. He proceeds to pour us a glass of St. Francis 2008 Zinfandel and orders the pasta to maintain his carbs for training.

Few people I knew can identify with Geoff's metabolic wonders. Most, however, will empathize with his life's journey from an out-of-work ad executive at a large ad agency, to picking up the pieces after a 3-month unemployment stint. Along the way Geoff made a transformation from a "slightly better than average ad agency account guy" to becoming one of the world's best recognized experts and thought leaders on any subject related to the Internet and digital advertising trends.

After working in the corporate advertising business for 15 years, the lay-off spurred Geoff to join forces with Sam Alfstad to do what many frustrated ad executives did at the time—he joined a small, boutique agency that was not part of an agency holding company. During these formative year's of the Internet, Geoff's clients increasingly requested help in developing a presence on the Web more than the traditional advertising services Geoff had built his early career learning. They began building web sites, having to learn html coding along the way. In trying to further his web skills, Geoff wound up spending a lot of his time researching the latest trends in web usage, e-commerce and online advertising. Both he and his clients wanted to know where this burgeoning medium was headed and what strategies they should adopt to take full advantage of it.

In the process, Geoff amassed a treasure trove of research which he began to aggregate and categorize. He was building a knowledge base that would turn out to be more valuable than the advertising web development services they provided. His partner asked him to write his own research report to leverage his growing knowledge. He created his organization's first white paper, which they sold to businesses for $295, thus thrusting Geoff into the first phase of the Thought Leadership process.

In 1999 they pivoted their business model and rechristened the firm as eMarketer. This started a business whose sole product is "thought leadership"—unique and actionable insights that helped businesses become smarter about the Web and in turn propelled eMarketer to explosive growth, prominence and profits. Being the first to aggregate already available research created a new business model that served to position Geoff as one of the most knowledgeable people on the planet on the topic of digital advertising trends. Geoff took advantage of a hole in the research market, met a huge demand for information and exploited it further with a new and valuable research service that businesses would pay by annual subscription, creating a predictable and renewable cash flow.

With his limitless energy and his love of showmanship he developed as an accomplished professional magician (a skill he began as a 12 year-old and honed throughout his lifetime), his presentations are a tour de force performance, combining his magician's sense of timing and human psychology with a deep knowledge of the industry and his facility with numbers (he is after all the son of a world renowned economist and mathematician).

Like most Thought Leaders, Geoff never planned for this phase of his life. The man and circumstances found their moment for which he was perfectly predisposed to fully exploit and in doing so, found himself doing "what he was always meant to do."

Not everyone can become a magician or develop showmanship presentation skills. Nor does one need Geoff's metabolic DNA to become a Thought Leader that leads to outsized profits and success for you and your business. But you can learn from Geoff's journey to success: Be open to new opportunities, combine your personal passion with your work, be relentless in learning everything about your chosen area of focused expertise, create content from that knowledge and monetize it through promotion and distribution.

PART I: **SAVANTS**

CHAPTER 1:
WHAT CLIENTS WANT

Take a moment and think about what you—a managing partner in a professional services firm—look for in other professionals. Let's get right to the point. If your child unfortunately required surgery, what qualities or attributes would you want in that surgeon? Let's extend this thinking to most professionals. What do you want from these professionals? Presuming that money is no obstacle and you need the services of a professional, what qualities or attributes would you look for in that individual or team?

Try the following exercise:

Step 1: Make a list of twenty professionals you know well who don't work in your firm or even in the same industry. These professionals can be ones your firm does business with, professionals you refer your clients to, or ones you employ personally.

Step 2: On a scale of one (not so good) to ten (great), rate how good they are in their chosen profession.

Step 3: Identify the qualities and attributes of those professionals you rate eight, nine or ten. What are the similarities and differences? Do any one or two characteristics stand out across all the top-rated professionals?

We've conducted this exercise at workshops and conferences with a wide range of audiences, from business owners to hedge fund managers to various professionals. Irrespective of the type of audience, we find very consistent answers. Always right up there in the top two or three is specialized knowledge or expertise—in other words, "brains." The people going through the exercise pretty unanimously want to work with highly talented and capable professionals.

"BRAINS"

Broadly speaking, let's characterize professional services firms as providing either "bodies" or "brains" (see Exhibit 1.1). The former is about increasing capacity to meet a need for (often standardized) resources that are likely to be temporary and can't be cost-effectively filled internally. The latter is about providing expertise, often incorporating customized elements. Professional services firms that provide either "bodies" or "brains" (or both) can supercharge their brands, and especially their business development efforts, by becoming thought leaders.

EXHIBIT 1.1: TYPES OF PROFESSIONALS

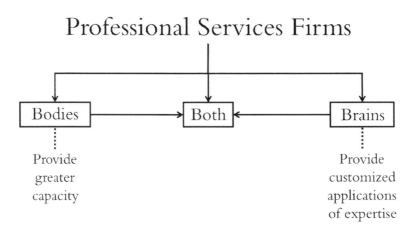

For those professional services firms that are focused on "brains," the importance of thought leadership is, or will become, increasingly decisive to the overall success of the firm (see *Coda: The Future of Profitable Brilliance*). For our purposes, we're going to concentrate our analysis, insights and guidelines on those professional services firms that are delivering high-levels of expertise—"brains."

Very likely, when you turn to professionals, you're interested in hiring the best available. Now, let's consider your firm's clients. Of the five choices below, which descriptor would best portray the professionals they work with?

- Inept.
- Limited.
- Adequate.
- Superior.
- Brilliant.

We suspect this question wasn't very hard to answer. Let's take another look at the matter. How important are the following things clients can get from professional services firms like yours?

- Obtaining the best possible solutions to their issues, concerns and problems.
- Working with the smartest professionals available.
- Getting the highest-quality advice cost-effectively.
- Having a good personal relationship with the professionals.
- Having "chemistry" with the professionals they employ.

No doubt buyers of professional services are interested in having a good relationship with their providers. However, when you consider why companies and individuals turn to professionals, it's often to address important concerns and problems. Therefore, it's pretty self-evident that they're looking for professionals with the best solutions and the ability to implement or help realize those solutions.

WHAT DO CLIENTS WANT?

To be very clear, consider the following questions:

- Why do clients buy the professional services your firm provides?
- What value do your clients believe they're receiving from your firm?
- What do your firm's clients require?

From our vantage point of working with many exceptional professional services firms as well as being one, when it comes to addressing often complex and always important issues, concerns and matters, given their druthers...

CLIENTS WANT BRILLIANCE

Let's look at it at a more granular level. Clients clearly want to engage the professional services firms that employ the foremost authorities in their respective areas of specialization. That means the professionals therein must be truly expert in their respective areas of specialization. So...

Clients want the individual professionals they employ to be savants.

This poses an interesting conundrum for the managing partners of professional services firm. In the quest to become a thought leader, a balance needs to be equalized between the firm, groups within the firms, teams within the groups and individuals. Nevertheless, it's fair to say that those professional services firms that stand out and are populated with well-recognized Savants are the likely preferred choice among potential clients as well as referral sources.

Operationally, brilliance alone is often insufficient to convert a prospect into a client and maintain the relationship. Other factors and variables regularly come into play. The one that we find most often cited is "chemistry."

WHAT ABOUT RAPPORT?

In developing thought leadership campaigns with professional services firms, we're sometimes questioned about the importance of personally connecting with clients. Although it's habitually self-evident that clients want to work with leading experts—Savants—we don't want to denigrate the importance of personally connecting. On the contrary, as we discuss in *Chapter 8: Productizing*, personal chemistry with clients and referral sources is almost always essential.

While research shows that rapport, for example, is not a reason the very wealthy say they select investment advisors, less obtrusive measurements repeatedly show that rapport is often a critical component of the decision-making process. Moreover, across the broad spectrum of professional services, chemistry or lack thereof between professionals and prospects is regularly a major factor in who gets the engagement.

Because many prospects as well as potential referral sources are incapable of evaluating the proficiencies of professional services firms (see *Chapter 4: The Case for Thought Leadership*), they have to presume that the professionals they're dealing with are top-notch. They are then making purchase decisions in part based on how they "click" with these professionals.

When deliverables such as a long-term corporate strategic plan or an estate plan for one of the super-rich (that is, individuals with a net worth of US$500 million or more) are largely impossible to validate, whom the prospect is most comfortable working with does indeed take on more importance. But the power of rapport should not be understated even in situations where deliverables can be readily assessed.

In the field of private investment management, for example, the wealthy can see how their portfolios are doing in real time. Even when the results of the professionals' expertise are evident and lacking, we've empirically demonstrated that high-quality relationship management can mitigate bad investment performance for an extensive period of time. In effect, even when wealthy investors are losing money, they can be motivated to continue working with substandard investment advisors who are especially adept at managing expectations (as opposed to assets).

The management of client expectations is exceptionally important across a wide and diverse spectrum of professional services. We've found that in situations where senior executives employ career or life coaches, rapport very often is more important than actually reaching the agreed-upon goals.

What's the implication of this? While prospects and clients are looking to work with the best authorities they can access, rapport between client and professional is most certainly a very potent factor in the selection process and even more important in the ongoing relationship. However, very often the underlying assumption is that professionals are fungible—assuming that they are generally very good at what they do, the ability of the professional to work well with the client is the differentiator.

Not diminishing the power of rapport, it is increasingly marginalized when one firm is a well-established thought leader standing above competitors. If clients need an audit, a consulting engagement, a legal assignment or some other professional service, by and large they want to know they're getting the best possible interpretations of the situation, the best possible answers and the best possible recommendations. Along the same lines, referral sources regularly want to make sure they're directing their clients to the very best, most talented professionals.

Prospects, clients and referral sources consider the thought leader to be the foremost authority, the undisputed expert. Across a wide range of professional services, we've consistently empirically demonstrated that the majority of clients are often willing to give up some, if not all, camaraderie in return for getting the best advice and solutions. It's even more evident with referral sources. Because of the risks to a business of making introductions to less than expert professionals, the perceived capabilities of those professionals consistently dominates the choice of whom to introduce clients to. When it comes right down to it, it's uncommon for clients or referral sources to sacrifice Brilliance for that "personal connection."

FOOD FOR THOUGHT

If clients want Brilliance, if they prefer a professional services firm that's replete with Savants who can make things happen, does your firm qualify? Without question, brilliance can be conceptualized as a range of genius, a spectrum of intelligence and operational abilities. As long as your firm's ability to deliver brilliant solutions matches the needs and wants of clients, and your clients perceive it that way, they will end up as advocates for your firm. The same logic holds for referral sources.

Doing the "right thing" and the absolute "best thing" for clients is a given. Assuming your professional services firm can deliver in that regard, your firm has to source prospects and motivate them to do business with you.

In today's hypercompetitive marketplace, you have to consider these things:
- How are you branding your firm?
- How are you sourcing clients?
- What types of marketing activities does your firm need to pursue to get better results than it is achieving today?

Becoming a thought leader can supercharge your firm's brand, resulting in a gushing pipeline of new high-caliber highly-financially rewarding clients. Becoming a thought leader, let alone a celebrity thought leader, dwarfs most other stand-alone marketing activities. And what's most intriguing is that any professional services firm can become a thought leader.

CHAPTER 2:
HIDDEN TALENTS OR TALENTED EXPERTS

For professional services firms, a number of characteristics can make their businesses exceptionally successful. That said, in the predominance of circumstances, clients want to work with professional services firms that are high-quality, top-of-the-line authorities in their respective areas of specialization (see *Chapter 1: What Clients Want*). Attaining high levels of expertise that can enable clients to effectively deal with problems and better their circumstances is incontrovertibly of critical importance. At the same time, as we'll see, competencies and know-how—even when the firm could objectively be defined as housing the most erudite professionals—are not necessarily enough to create a highly successful professional services firm.

In our view, absolutely essential to your firm's success is the ability to access high-quality prospects that are strongly inclined to do business with your firm. No matter how technically proficient your partners and associates are, without appropriately motivated and well-paying clients, your firm will not flourish. If no one is going to take advantage of the Savants enclosed in the cubicles and offices at your professional services firm, then your firm will wither away, if not disintegrate or implode.

While many other factors and traits are very important to business success, sourcing clients has to be—for nearly all professional services firms—at the very top of the list. Simply put, without clients there is no professional services firm.

With respect to cultivating desirable clients, you need to be able to wisely answer two critical questions:

Question 1: Compared to your competitors, how expert is your firm?

Question 2: Compared to your competitors, how good is your firm at business development?

As we have pointed out, many factors have to be in place to sustain an astounding professional services business. Nevertheless, the ability to source preferred clients is unassailably essential. We've found an all too pervasive and debilitating drawback infecting a great many professional services firms in their inability to answer these two questions.

To get a better understanding of this matter, let's consider the matter from another direction. What's the actual relationship between expertise and business development?

THE ROLE OF EXPERTISE

In working with some exceptionally capable professional services firms jam-packed with exceptionally gifted and sometimes genius-level professionals, we repeatedly find an interesting and potentially problematic misunderstanding. The managing partners as well as the rank-and-file professionals at these firms frequently equate their potential business success almost solely with their mastery of specialized material. For example, it's often the norm that:

- Trusts and estate lawyers define their level of prospective success based on their knowledge of tax law and their ability to apply this knowledge on behalf of clients.
- Investment advisors define their potential success based on their understanding of markets and their skills at managing assets.

- Accountants strongly identify their financial opportunities with their ability to navigate and address the complexities of the tax code.
- Architects refer to their drafting and related skills as their core ability and the one that will bring in clients.
- Executive search professionals often refer to their networks as the reason for candidates to select them over their competitors.

Consider any type of professional: What would he or she identify as instrumental to his or her success? Although expertise is the politically correct answer, what's more insightful is that we've very consistently found that deep in their hearts, professionals believe this is the answer. They sincerely equate their technical proficiencies with the success of their practices.

Unfortunately for these professionals, they're often badly mistaken. Technical capabilities—even at a genius level—do not automatically convert into business accomplishments. While we always advocate exceptional competency, such levels of proficiency do not always translate into financially successful professional services firms.

It's great when the professional services firm is able to marshal Savants with considerable support resources to provide top-of-the-line solutions to clients. It's all well and good when that professional is really an authority in his or her field.

But it's a major, insidious and potentially profoundly debilitating problem when managing partners automatically link the technical proficiencies of the professionals in their firms with anticipated financial accomplishments. It's not that technical proficiencies are not crucial. It's what clients are seeking (see *Chapter 1: What Clients Want*) and what they certainly deserve. It's just that very commonly, even genius-level knowledge and accompanying skill is not enough to make a professional services firm a flourishing enterprise. Because this view that expertise equals business success is pretty rampant among professional services firms, a grave number of them never achieve the fiscal promise that seems to hover just beyond their reach.

EXPERTISE VERSUS BRAND

The expectation that merited high-caliber expertise alchemically transforms into business success and personal wealth is plainly fallacious. What we have here is a structurally derived myth borne from the very processes and means for creating and populating a technically high-caliber professional services firm. The "we're good" argument has become a parody of a cliché. Among prospects and referral sources, it's considered a given.

Going back to those two critical questions, let us pose a third: **Question 3:** What is more important to cultivating sensational clients, your firm's expertise or your firm's professional brand?

Even after reading to this point, you might conclude that expertise trumps brand. In a perfect—nay, rational—world, you would be correct. However, the world we inhabit is far from rational (let's not even touch on the idea of perfection).

When it comes to professional services firms and business development, a high-quality and powerful brand can displace or overshadow expertise nearly every time. Keep in mind that we're strictly addressing the matter of business development. We're not addressing your firm's ability to capably and effectively provide top-notch professional services. As we've said, we are very intense advocates of exceptional competency. But we readily recognize that such competence does not necessarily correlate with effective business development. At the same time, we're pretty sure that you're familiar with many fairly successful professionals who are not all that expert or even that good.

THE EXPERTISE/BRAND MATRIX

Let's examine the logic of brand superiority by using the expertise/brand matrix (see Exhibit 2.1). For didactic simplicity, let's divide both expertise and brand into two levels—high and low. This produces four quadrants inhabited by four types of professional services firms.

EXHIBIT 2.1: EXPERTISE/BRAND MATRIX

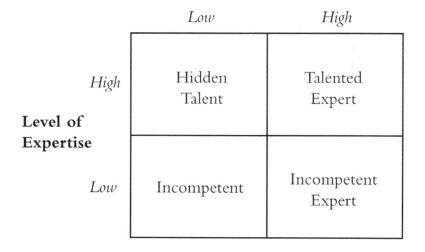

Degree of Professional Brand Equity

	Low	High
High	Hidden Talent	Talented Expert
Low	Incompetent	Incompetent Expert

Level of Expertise

Talented Expert. A high level of expertise coupled with a strong professional brand makes your professional services firm a

Talented Expert. Your firm is as adept as any of its competitors, and the "right people"—existing clients, prospects, referral sources and intermediaries—know who you are and what you are capable of doing extremely well.

The "talented" component of the descriptor means that your firm will do an exceptional job for clients. The "expert" component means that your firm will have the opportunity to do so. In this matrix, this is the best place for your professional services firm to be.

Hidden Talent. What happens if your professional services firm truly has a high level of expertise but lacks a meaningful brand? It's not well recognized for its knowledge and capabilities. If this is the case, your firm is a Hidden Talent.

Given the opportunity to work for a high-caliber client, the firm will do an exceptional job. The big complication is in sourcing that high-caliber client. Potential clients are unaware of, or have a limited view of, your professional services firm. This results in your firm periodically—or worse, frequently—not being in the running to win a prospect's business. The same can be said of referral sources and intermediaries.

Incompetents. Moving to the bottom left quadrant of our matrix, we refer to those professional services firms who lack expertise and lack a professional brand as Incompetents. There's little doubt that the professionals in these firms can scrounge out a living or slightly better, but it's unlikely they'll accomplish very much. Their ability to source new business is dreadfully limited.

Incompetent Experts. The scariest quadrant houses the Incompetent Experts. These are professional services firms with a very solid and attractive brand in the right circles—clients, prospects, referral sources and intermediaries. The fact that they're not very capable is not a deterrent to their ability to generate a lot of new business and consequently tremendous pecuniary success.

A lack of real technical capabilities doesn't pose an obstacle to very effective business development efforts when the people in the right circles believe the professional services firm is loaded with Savants in command of state-of-the-art knowledge, coupled with an adroit ability to implement—reality be damned!

Based on our experience in working with some of the leading professional services firms worldwide, an all too common misunderstanding needs correction:

Being recognized by decision-makers as an expert and actually being an expert is not necessarily the same thing.

This life-and-business lesson, we've found, is very hard for many managing partners at professional services firms to accept. Not surprisingly, it's sometimes an even harder lesson for the professionals in the firms to learn.

Herein, we're going to do our best to ensure that when you finish reading, you understand that exceptional expertise, while absolutely essential, is often insufficient for significant business success. Being selectively famous is repeatedly an essential that converts into sourcing new high-quality business (see *Chapter 5: Fame, Then Fortunes*).

High-caliber prospects and clients engage leading specialists—professionals they perceive as experts. Referral sources and intermediaries turn to renowned industry authorities—professionals they perceive as experts. This perception is predominantly the deciding dynamic when it comes to the vast majority of highly effective business development activities for professional services firms that deliver "brains."

When it comes to very effective business development, the Talented Experts and the Incompetent Experts pretty much occupy the same playing field. Why is this the case? It's really quite simple. When it comes to professional services—complex knowledge-based specializations—clients and prospects, as well as their other advisors and confidants, are regularly incapable of accurately evaluating the legitimate expertise and capabilities of most professionals (see *Chapter 4: The Case for Thought Leadership*).

It's the rare professional in the investment advisory firm, for instance, who is able to determine whether the life insurance program put together by a top-of-the-line life insurance boutique is truly optimal. Along the same lines, few professionals within a property and casualty firm understand the components and mechanics that go into a complex three-party loan agreement, including accurately addressing all the loan covenants. The technology consultant is usually hard-pressed to understand the processes, tools and techniques of the life coach.

The same logic holds true when it comes to many introductions from referral sources. It's generally the case that the referral source depends more on a professional services firm's overall reputation and recognition as an industry authority in making introductions, as opposed to critically evaluating the depth and breadth of that firm's expertise.

THE COMPETITION

Without question, several additional factors can prove decisive in accessing high-caliber clients. Because of the risks to their business if a firm "blows up" their top clients, we would argue that most potential referral sources are highly disinclined to refer others to Incompetents. However, without direct experience with a professional services firm, a potential referral source can rarely tell if that firm is truly a top expert. So we're back to the importance of a professional services firm's brand equity in developing new business.

For the most part, if a professional services firm neglects to develop and enhance its brand, that firm is going to be limited—to say the least—when it comes to building a book of exceptional clients. Commonly, over time many of these professional services firms can develop a brand. The issue is, will it be an effective brand that will meaningfully enhance the firm's ability to effectively source high-caliber clients?

It's not much of a stretch to say that among the panoply of diverse professional services firms, there are a greater number of Incompetent Experts than there are Talented Experts. There are also likely to be many more Hidden Talents than Experts. And in many professions, there are very likely more Incompetents than any of the other three types.

No matter how you assess and evaluate the competitive environment, when it comes to building a book of high-caliber clients, the Experts dominate. The Incompetents are seldom a threat, save for the rare client or two or three. And you generally need not worry very much about the Hidden Talents, as they tend to stay hidden. Like the professionals housed in the Incompetents, the professionals housed in the Hidden Talents will, now and again, fall into some very good business opportunities, but it's a somewhat random and erratic progression. Hence, the bona fide competition is among the Incompetent Experts and the Talented Experts. What's so interesting is that they're generally more or less on an equal footing.

DIAGNOSTIC

Let's assume your professional services firm is actually replete with some of the foremost authorities in their fields—Savants. When we've run events such as conferences and workshops, and we've asked who, in the audience of professionals, is in the top 10% of their profession, nearly everyone (if not everyone) raises their hand. It's easy to say you or your firm is an expert. But when you say this, who believes you?

Your professional services firm's positioning as an expert does not necessarily depend on what you believe or proclaim, but rather on what your clients, prospects and prospective referral sources and intermediaries believe. Going through the following simple diagnostic can help you clarify the extent to which others may perceive your firm as an expert.

Step 1: Write down how you and your partners would describe your firm to prospects and prospective referral sources. Make sure to briefly identify your expertise.

Step 2: Identify five high-caliber clients as well as five referral sources.

Step 3: Write down how each of the ten decision-makers would describe you to a prospect you want to cultivate. Write down what each one would say is your firm's area(s) of expertise.

Step 4: For the descriptions you detailed in Step 3, provide some proof that your assessments are correct. Otherwise, reevaluate your responses to Step 3.

Step 5: If there's a disconnect between Step 1 and Step 3, it's very likely that while your firm might indeed be expert, it's a Hidden Talent. We've found that for most professional services firms, that is the case.

If your firm is like the majority of professional services firms, its brand and positioning could do with some polishing. This may have nothing to do with the technical capabilities it can bring to a client—your firm's technical expertise. However, as we see, being an unknown expert—a Hidden Talent—might result in a satisfactory living for the professionals at the firm, but it does relatively little if your goal is to build a very successful business. As we'll detail, the thought leadership process can dramatically contribute to your firm transitioning from a Hidden Talent to a Talented Expert (see Exhibit 2.2).

EXHIBIT 2.2: FROM HIDDEN TALENTS TO TALENTED EXPERT

What's also quite telling and extremely important to recognize is that the thought leadership process can also dramatically contribute to a professional services firm's transition from Incompetent to Incompetent Expert (see Exhibit 2.3). Becoming a thought leader is principally all about gaining recognition as one of the foremost authorities in a specific field of expertise. The fact that even professional services firms that lack know-how and the capacity to implement can become thought leaders makes it all the more difficult for the firm housing truly talented professionals to stand out.

EXHIBIT 2.3: FROM INCOMPETENT TO INCOMPETENT EXPERT

FOOD FOR THOUGHT

One of the most pervasive and persistent problems many professional services firms face is the presumption that being good at what you do is the answer to meaningful and extensive business development—and if being technically good is the answer, then being really technically good is even better.

These firms believe that somehow clients and referral source just need to see how good the professionals at the firm are, and that alone will then drive business development. Strangely enough, this point of view comes up often in meetings we've attended with managing partners. In this scenario, what the managing partners are actually doing is putting the onus for recognizing their firm's capabilities, skills and talents on the shoulders of clients and referral sources. As we'll see in *Chapter 4: The Case for Thought Leadership*, it's an untenable position, as so few people outside a particular profession can adequately judge the quality of work in that field.

There's no question, meanwhile, that recognition of your professional services firm as an authority in select fields can prove extremely profitable. This stature can readily result in more effectively getting repeat business from existing clients. It can make your professional services firm the go-to choice among high-caliber prospects. It can also be instrumental in motivating referral sources to consistently and actively send their best clients your way. It can be central in getting business through intermediaries.

It's absolutely the responsibility of the professional services firm to create the appropriate brand equity. As much as possible, your professional services firm's brand should convey that it's a Talented Expert—that extremely wise and capable professionals within the firm can do a great job of providing viable and actionable solutions. There are a small number of particularly powerful ways in which you can accomplish this objective. One of the most efficacious ways for your firm to be seen as a Talented Expert is by becoming a thought leader.

INTERLUDE: MR. BtoB

RICK SEGAL, PRESIDENT WORLDWIDE, GYRO

Spend time with Rick Segal and you can "see" the light bulbs going off in his head as he speaks. His articulation of new and actionable paradigms is accentuated by his signature look—beard and bow-tie. He is an extraordinary synthesizer of ideas and master of formulating and articulating those ideas into business communication strategies. He is after all "Mr. BtoB", recognized in his industry as a thought leader on all things related to advertising to business decision makers.

Today he is the Worldwide President and Chief Practice Officer for gyro, the world's largest business to business advertising agency after having founded HSR Advertising in Cincinnati in 1981. He and his partners Mike Hensley and Tom Rentschler built this fledgling rust-belt ad agency into a fast growing powerhouse. With the infusion of private equity to capitalize their growth, they began an M&A tear over the past several years that lead them to their current position of preeminence around the world.

But it wasn't always thus. True he was born to be noticed—he was the master of ceremonies at his kindergarten pageant where he began his penchant for bow-ties—Rick had to work hard to earn his "thought leader" stripes. He is truly a self-made man. While he didn't exactly grow up on the wrong side of the tracks, his upbringing was at least along side them with modest, middle-class means. Like many with an entrepreneur's mind set, he chose not to go to college. Instead, he went to school on life and became a quick study of human behavior. He learned the business of communication and persuasion through campaign politics after having the good fortune to work on the election campaign for a Republican congressional candidate in 1970 at the astonishing age of 12 (his life-long passion and savvy for the political realm remains to this day).

The career light-bulb went off for Rick when he came to the realization that few people in business as he put it "know what they're doing." They either couldn't articulate the reasons why their businesses succeed or fail or worse, much to his naive amazement, they simply didn't know. He came to the conclusion that a solid business could be built around that delta–the classic space for a consultative service firm to operate. He built his own expertise by reading anything and everything having to do with his client's business–every trade magazine, every newsletter, every product brochure about his clients and their competitors–an exercise few people have the interest or stamina to engage in.

Rick Segal is now a popular speaker at industry events and is coveted as a board member for many local and national industry organizations and associations. Here are Rick's five steps to thought leadership:

1) Never stop going to school (read, read, read, listen, listen, and listen).

2) Ride the wave before others do–formulate your "world view" on your topic of expertise, write it down and continually practice articulating it every chance you get, then modify and evolve it as you see others respond to it.

3) Pursue and accept memberships in industry associations and groups.

4) Never turn down an opportunity to speak in front of those groups and relevant conferences.

5) Promote yourself–write a blog, participate in social media do an interview with local media.

The key to Rick and gyro's success is that the worldwide advertising agency he now helps to run leverages Rick's thought leader status for above category norms for growth and profitability.

PART II: IN THE LINE OF MONEY

CHAPTER 3:
WHAT IS A THOUGHT LEADER?

There's a lot of talk among professionals—especially those managing professional services firms—on the value and advantages of being a thought leader. The complication is that professionals freely and easily use the term to address various positions and roles with varying business implications.

When you think of the term thought leader, what comes to mind? Before proceeding further in this chapter, it might be useful to write down your answers. We've also found it very advantageous to identify how the other managing partners in your firm would answer the question. We hypothesize that you won't find a great deal of consensus among the partners.

With all the definitional dispersion around the term, as a starting point it's usually very worthwhile to define for yourself and your firm just what a thought leader is and, sometimes more important, what a thought leader is not. The following exercise can prove useful:

Step 1: Write down five professional services firms you consider to be thought leaders.

Step 2: Identify for each of these firms the fields of specialization where they're thought leaders.

Step 3: For each of these firms, indicate the reason(s) you consider them thought leaders. Be as specific as possible in citing validating proofs.

Step 4: From these examples, determine the pattern that you consider to be evidence of thought leadership.

Step 5: Have other managing partners at your firm go through Steps 1 through 4. Determine if there is any overlap between yourself and your partners.

Step 6: Examine the patterns you uncovered, and define how you and your partners define thought leadership.

You're likely to find that some professionals take a very expansive view of the term, wrapping internal strategy and corporate culture into their definition. Other professionals are more constrained in their definition. Based on your definition, take another moment to consider the value that your firm gets as a thought leader, or that it would accrue if it became one.

The way we conceptualize and define thought leadership shows the potentially exponential payback to being a thought leader. In fact, that exponential payback is very much the focal point of our thinking about thought leadership.

What's essential is that your professional services firm cannot possibly be a thought leader unless it is capitalizing on its dramatically enhanced brand equity. This requires that you know—in advance of launching any thought leadership initiative—how your professional services firm is likely to gain financially. When we conduct such economic analyses and monitor results, we're aiming for significant (regularly astounding) financial gains (see *Chapter 9: Monetizing*).

A THOUGHT LEADER

Based on decades of working with professional services firms in assisting them to become thought leaders, we have a two-part definition of what constitutes a thought leader (see Exhibit 3.1):

DEFINITION—PART ONE

A thought leader is a professional services firm that prospects, clients, referral sources, intermediaries and even competitors recognize as one of the foremost authorities in selected areas of specialization, resulting in its being the go-to firm for said expertise.

Considering the title of this book, what we're talking about in Part One of the definition is "brilliance." It's the expertise that clients are going to professional services firms for (see *Chapter 1: What Clients Want*).

What's essential to understand is that brilliance doesn't exist in a vacuum, and it's a total waste of time to debate whether it is authentic. Brilliance is a function of acclaim, created where others bestow the accolades. In this regard, becoming a thought leader is a critically effective means of transitioning from a Hidden Talent to a Talented Expert.

We now move to the second part, the commercial component of the definition:

DEFINITION—PART TWO

A thought leader is a professional services firm that significantly profits from being recognized as such.

EXHIBIT 3.1: DEFINITION OF A THOUGHT LEADER

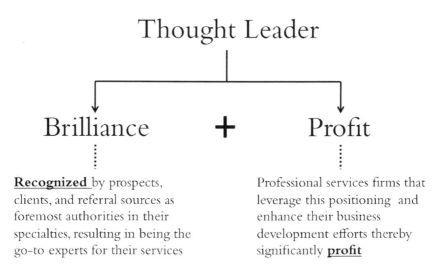

Thought Leader

Brilliance + **Profit**

Recognized by prospects, clients, and referral sources as foremost authorities in their specialties, resulting in being the go-to experts for their services

Professional services firms that leverage this positioning and enhance their business development efforts thereby significantly **profit**

By design, professional services firms are guns for hire. By and large, their objective is to do a top-notch job for their clients and (whether their managing partners admit it or not) get well paid for their services. This is only possible when professional services firms are able to garner and maintain high-caliber clients who are able and motivated to compensate them fairly. Being a thought leader is very much about making money—and there are two principal ways to accomplish this (see *Chapter 9: Monetizing*).

Let's consider a tax accounting firm that wants to become a thought leader. A new law comes out that will have a dramatic effect on how to address the depreciation of certain corporate assets. For the tax accounting firm to appear as a thought leader, the tax partners have to do a lot more than merely regurgitate the new law. However, in most situations with professionals, simply repeating the basics tends to be the norm.

To become a thought leader, the tax accounting firm needs to do a deep dive concerning the new law. The partners must determine just how the law will impact various companies. Furthermore, the tax accountants must develop distinctive insights and actionable planning strategies based on the new law. There have to be recommendations attached to the analysis that can prove beneficial to the impacted companies. It's of critical importance that the tax accounting firm communicates that it is the go-to expert concerning these distinctive insights and actionable strategies.

Many professionals stop here and declare themselves thought leaders. This is a very serious mistake. Being selectively renowned can be very rewarding, but being wealthy as well is immensely better. Without question, this is a very capitalist perspective. However, considering our affiliation with Forbes, it shouldn't be surprising.

For a professional services firm to be a thought leader, it's especially critical that the firm monetize its state-of-the-art thinking by increasing its ability to source, work with and thereby profit from its desired clientele. In effect, as we're conceptualizing the role, being a thought leader includes the ability to garner radically above-average returns on effort.

While there are many ways to define success, we take a very mercantile approach to the matter (see *Appendix A: Money Rules*). For us, the financial health of the professional services firm determines success in these situations. The more profitable the firm is, the better. Of course, all sorts of factors impact the profitability of a professional services firm. Business development is just one piece of this complex and shifting puzzle. Nevertheless, it's the piece that forcefully influences the viability of probably all professional services firms, and it's the piece that being a thought leader greatly strengthens and improves upon.

FOOD FOR THOUGHT

In working with many managing partners at various professional services firms, we find that our business-development, very revenue-oriented view of thought leadership can be off-putting. It's not that they don't want their firms to make money; it's more about our directness in saying that's the goal. The logic falls along the same lines as the thinking that clients and referral sources should come use their services because the professionals at the firm are top-notch (see *Chapter 2: Hidden Talents or Talented Experts*).

Compared to many other definitions, our definition of a thought leader is clearly quite narrow. Furthermore, most definitions don't share our strong emphasis on the requirement that the professional services firm must be financially profitable to be a thought leader, no matter how many phenomenal insights it shares.

We make no apologies for our revenue-oriented view. For the thought leadership campaigns we've assisted with, we can regularly unmistakably demonstrate the considerable return on investment to the professional services firms. The goal of generating new engagements with better and better clients banishes any questions about the real value of being a thought leader.

CHAPTER 4:
THE CASE FOR THOUGHT LEADERSHIP

To get a better perspective on why so many professional services firms are striving to become thought leaders, let's break down the multiple benefits of achieving this stature. When and where does being a thought leader really matter? It's certainly not for every professional services firm. In considering the following questions, you can determine the extent to which being a thought leader can prove beneficial and worthwhile for your firm.

- Would your firm profit from being able to access significantly more qualified and motivated clients for its services?
- Are the services of your firm "commodities" that are relatively easily interchangeable with those of competitors?
- Does your firm face significant competition for high-caliber clients?
- Are the clients of your firm somewhat or highly cost-conscious, if not cost-sensitive?
- Would your firm considerably profit by speeding up the sales cycle?
- Would it serve the bottom line of your firm to have considerably more solid and expansive relationships with its better current clients?

If the answer to all six of these questions was "yes," then your professional services firm would considerably benefit from being a thought leader. Even if only half the answers were "yes," then your professional services firm would still considerably benefit.

It's a very rare case in which a professional services firm would not gain a substantial competitive advantage from being a thought leader. As we've emphasized, when done well, being a thought leader results in substantial monetary rewards. That's not to say that each and every professional services firm should strive to be a thought leader in all its areas of practice. However, if a firm carefully evaluates its business models and selects those practice areas in which it wants to blossom fiscally, being a thought leader in those specialties is very likely the answer.

THE BENEFITS TO BEING A THOUGHT LEADER

A firm needs to evaluate strategic, operational and financial issues in determining if, where and how to become a thought leader. Nevertheless, if the capabilities and resources as well as the managerial leadership are available, very few—if any— professional services firms would not come out way ahead by becoming a thought leader. Let's drill down a little and consider how this option delivers.

Increase access to qualified clients. Most professional services firms want to spend their time courting decidedly desirable high-caliber clients. Because thought leadership has a tremendous marketing pull, when it is executed adroitly it results in a large increase in prospective eager—and appropriate—clients.

- What would happen to the success of your professional services firm if it were able to create a pipeline of high-caliber clients and keep it filled?
- What is your firm doing today to build this pipeline?
- How would becoming a thought leader help build and fill this pipeline?

Commoditized services. The services of one accomplished professional services firm are not inherently different from those of equally capable competitors. In these situations, being the thought leader can cut through the clutter of undifferentiated offerings.

- Would you consider the expertise provided by your professional services firm to be at all commoditized?
- What is your firm doing to differentiate itself where its offerings are highly fungible?
- How would being a thought leader differentiate your firm and its services from the panoply of competitors?

Relatively low barriers of entry. When it's relatively easy to compete and profitable to do so, then competition is likely to increase. As more professional services firms target many of the same clients, the thought leader is the firm that's best able to stand apart from and above the miasma.

- How difficult is it for other professional services firms to focus on the same high-caliber clientele your firm is interested in?
- How easy is it for other professionals (including your current partners) to set up shop and compete with your firm?
- How would your firm, as a thought leader, mitigate the threat of current and new competitors?

Cost-sensitive clients. Where the purchasers of the professional services are concerned about costs and can shop around—as is most often the case—the thought leaders are best positioned to charge a premium or at least higher prices than most competitors. Moreover, established adept thought leaders are better able to maintain their pricing structure in the face of stern competition, even with most cost-conscious clients.

- Do the prospects and clients of your professional services firm ever shop around to lower their bills?
- Have your firm's clients ever questioned their bills and negotiated to pay less?
- How would being a thought leader enable your firm to regularly charge premium prices and get them?

Mitigated sales cycle. It's not uncommon for there to be a gap between recognition of a service need and obtaining the engagement. The larger this gap, the greater the costs, including opportunity costs and the deferred revenues to the professional services firm. The expertise that prospects attribute to the thought leader regularly converts into a comparatively shorter sales cycle.

- Has the length of time increased between your firm's initial meeting with a prospect and turning that prospect into a client?
- What are the consequences of a longer and more involved sales cycle for the finances of your firm?
- How would becoming a thought leader help close the gap between connecting with a prospect and converting that prospect into a client?

Stronger relationships with existing clients. It's highly probable that competitors are perpetually wooing your professional services firm's better clients. Being a thought leader communicates to current clients that they are working with one of the foremost industry authorities. Consequently, it can powerfully reinforce a client's decision to do business with your professional services firm, thereby boxing out competitors. This also regularly converts into continued and expanded business with these clients.

- Are competitors soliciting your professional services firm's better clients?

- What would be the impact on your firm of these clients shifting allegiances and firms?
- How would being a thought leader enable your firm to help ensure the continuity and expansion of these prosperous relationships?

These benefits clearly overlap and produce a self-reinforcing pattern. While the benefits discussed are certainly all possible when the professional services firm is a thought leader, what we identify as most crucial is the monetary result that is obtainable by acknowledgment as one of the leading experts in a practice area. What does all this mean? Again, from our perspective, it's all about business development.

THOUGHT LEADERSHIP AND BUSINESS DEVELOPMENT

As we voiced in *Chapter 3: What Is a Thought Leader?* and have repeated in this chapter, the principal motivation for a professional services firm to be a thought leader is, or should be, primarily if not exclusively about business development (see Exhibit 4.1).

EXHIBIT 4.1: THE LOGIC UNDERPINNING THOUGHT LEADERSHIP

Thought Leader = Business Development

For existing clients, the value is in maintaining the relationships plus winning new engagements with these clients. Prospects readily turn to thought leaders for reasons we'll specify. And, most important, referral sources prefer introducing their best clients to thought leaders for a number of reasons. Intermediaries are also motivated to work with thought leaders. Let's take a closer look at each of these four opportunities.

Client retention and new engagements. Your professional services firm's existing clients are great sources of continued and often additional business. A large part of retaining clients is meeting—and preferably exceeding—their expectations with respect to the services your firm delivers. However, even when your firm did an exceptional job, for many clients there are ofttimes questions about whom to turn to for professional services the next time.

Being a thought leader is like a warm down blanket on a bitterly cold night—it's an extra layer of protection. It positions your professional services firm as the leading expert, and individual and corporate clients do prefer to work with the best whenever possible.

Being a thought leader is proof positive that you are the best or, in the worst case, one of a very few that are the best. By providing the appropriate thought leadership products to your firm's current clients and conducting the proper follow-up, you're reinforcing and strengthening your firm's relationship with these clients. In addition, you're potentially setting the stage to pick up new engagements from these clients.

Prospects. The prospects of your professional services firm, given their druthers without other mitigating circumstances, almost universally prefer working with thought leaders. A number of factors are often critical when prospects decide on professional services firms, and these factors favor thought leaders (see Exhibit 4.2).

- *Complexity of the professional services being delivered.* The more complicated and involved the offerings, the more prospects are disposed to turn to recognized state-of-the-art authorities. Thought leaders are, by definition, the renowned experts in their respective fields.

- *Intangibility of the professional services.* The harder it is to directly evaluate and compare offerings, the more appealing thought leaders become. Prospects can't "see and touch" many professional services, which translates into a reliance on established well-known specialists.

- *Level of embedded risks to the client.* The more detrimental and potentially adverse choosing the wrong professional can prove, the more effort prospects will make to find what they would define as the best. They often see thought leaders as the professionals most suited to provide the requisite solutions.

- *Difficult learning curve with respect to the professional services.* The less the prospects are able to study up on the mechanics and dynamics of the professional services they're acquiring, the more they prefer to work with the foremost authorities in the field. These foremost authorities are the thought leaders.

EXHIBIT 4.2: THOUGHT LEADERSHIP AND THE FACTORS IMPACTING PROSPECTS' DECISION MAKING

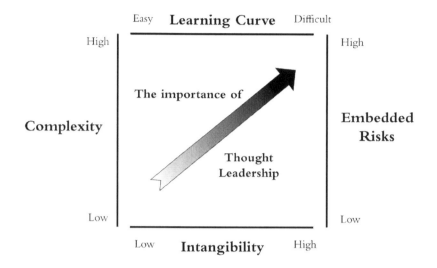

While we decomposed the discussion of prospect decision-making into four factors for educational purposes, it's important to recognize that the factors interrelate and strengthen each other. These factors all tie together, with additional ones, in that prospects are looking to mitigate risk in addressing situations where they have limited understanding and knowledge, but often intense needs and preferences. Moreover, due to the very nature of professional services, prospects are going to have to rely on the advice and direction provided by the professional. As a thought leader, your firm is adroitly positioned to capitalize on the risk-mitigation decision-making characteristic of the vast majority of prospects.

Introductions from referral sources. For many types of professional services, being introduced to qualified prospects by other professionals is the optimal or near optimal business development strategy (see *Appendix B: Creating Strategic Partnerships with Referral Sources*). What is demonstrably clear is that for the referral source, making such introductions is often a high-risk endeavor. Simply put, if the referral does not work out well, the credibility and judgment of the referral source comes into question. As professional services are all about credibility of judgment, the referral source can come out a very big loser. Making an introduction to a thought leader mitigates the risk (see Exhibit 4.3).

EXHIBIT 4.3: MITIGATING REFERRAL RISKS

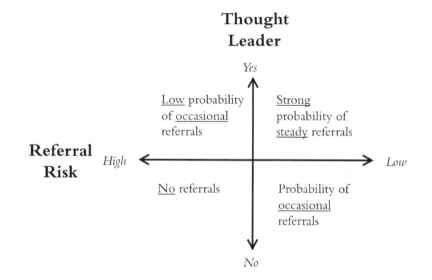

For this reason, we've found that many professionals are very reticent about making referrals. Your dual-impact brand (see *Chapter 5: Fame, Then Fortunes*), powered by high-caliber thought leadership products and directed through a strategic partnering process, can create a tsunami of new business opportunities. Thought leadership makes it increasingly easy for referral sources to refer to you, for the following reasons:

- *Validation of your firm's expertise.* The fact that referral sources can point to your stature and standing as a thought leader enables them to, with greater confidence and legitimacy, comfortably and actively recommend your professional services firm to their clients.
- *More easily communicate your firm's expertise.* When making introductions, it's not uncommon for the referral sources to not be very practiced at making the case for your firm. Enabling the referral sources to use and leverage your thought leadership products can eliminate this problem.
- *Currency for qualified introductions.* Thought leadership products that your firm develops to make the referral sources more successful in their own right are a very powerful form of currency. They can be highly effective in motivating the referrals sources to proactively identify and introduce their qualified clients to your firm.

Being a thought leader in alignment with your firm's dual-impact branding strategy is a very potent lubricant to facilitate new business. However, to create a forever-filled pipeline of new high-caliber clients for your professional services firm, you'll need to foster strategic partnerships with high-quality referral sources (see *Appendix B: Creating Strategic Partnerships with Referral Sources*).

It's also possible to create a more potent alignment of strategic partners. We refer to each of these loosely structured but tightly allied sets of supportive professionals as elite professional networks. In each of these networks, a number of the members need to be thought leaders in their respective fields (see *Appendix C: Elite Professional Networks*).

Intermediaries. In a number of circumstances, professional services firms are actually wholesaling their expertise. These firms are marketing their professional services to and through intermediaries who are likely to be other professionals. Here, we're talking about a much tighter relationship than sourcing new clients through referral sources. In this situation, we're explicitly dealing with intermediaries who are using your firm's services with their clients.

This is very well exemplified in the financial services business, where money management firms such as mutual fund companies market their investment products through panoply of financial advisors. The practice has become so institutionalized that it's referred to as value-added wholesaling, and quite a number of mutual fund companies and similar organizations have units dedicated to developing value-added (a.k.a. thought leadership) products. While the quality of the thought leadership products that a firm provides strongly influences success in motivating financial advisors to use certain investment products over others, the quality of the investment products are sometimes (but far from always) more of a determinant.

Becoming a value-added wholesaler of professional services, though pervasive in the financial services arena, is less established in many other corners of the professional services universe. That said, we are confident that with greater and greater commoditization of professional services, mounting competition and ever more discriminating clients and referral sources, augmented by evolving communications capabilities and computer-driven analytics, value-added wholesaling will become much more wide-spread and expected. Some professional services firms will seek to benefit disproportionately from this trend, which will require becoming thought leaders.

To wholesale professional services through intermediaries, a firm has to implement the thought leadership process and over-lay a more complex business model. Because of the additional layers of operational and structural complexity that's inherent in working through intermediaries, our focus in this treatise will be on referral sources.

ADDITIONAL BENEFITS TO BEING A THOUGHT LEADER

The way we think about the benefits of thought leadership is that they're tightly connected, if not synonymous with, business development. For us, it's all about:

- Helping to maintain and expand relationships with existing clients.
- Generating new business opportunities in the form of new clients.

However, other advantages will likely accrue to your professional services firm as a thought leader. The biggest added advantage falls under the broad heading of talent management (see Exhibit 4.4). The following are some of the benefits beyond business development for professionals leveraging their firm's thought leadership position:

- *Staying state-of-the-art.* With the changes that perpetually trans-verse all knowledge-intensive environments, professionals are forever students. To stay current with, let alone ahead of, competitors requires a near-religious commitment to upgrad-ing their skills and knowledge. Professional services firms that are thought leaders strongly support this learner mentality.

- *Increased competencies.* Expanding from the previous point, professionals not only have to stay up-to-date, but at many times need to become proficient in related relevant specializations. The professionals within the walls of a firm that's a thought leader in select areas greatly benefit by developing new germane skills and knowledge that can enhance their business and careers.

- *Better able to recruit and retain top talent.* By and large, besides wanting to become increasingly more adept, professionals want to be associated with and be a part of more capable firms. To the extent that they have to source business, they also regularly appreciate their firms being strongly market oriented, thereby providing them with meaningful support and related opportunities. The professional services firm that's a thought leader can more effectively attract and hold high-quality professionals.

EXHIBIT 4.4: THOUGHT LEADERSHIP AND TALENT MANAGEMENT

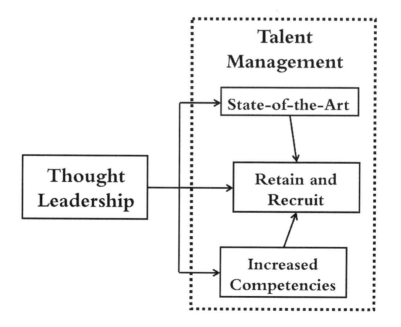

A critical success factor of any professional services firms is the quality of its professionals. A firm can powerfully leverage its status as a thought leader to attract and motivate truly talented and capable professionals. Concurrently, it can wisely employ its intellectual capital, thought leadership content and thought leadership products to raise the capabilities and proficiencies of its professionals. With astute, insightful and forward-thinking management, this creates an environment where the professional services firm's thought leadership status continues to rise and where the expertise of the professionals at the firm reaches greater heights. It can be a very synergistic arrangement (see Exhibit 4.5).

EXHIBIT 4.5: SYNERGY

Thought Leadership

Creates and expands opportunities to develop and execute thought leadership initiatives

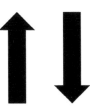

Enhances recruitment, retention and professional development

Talent Management

FOOD FOR THOUGHT

Being a thought leader is very beneficial to any professional services firm. A firm that's a thought leader gains quite a few distinct advantages. From our perspective, thought leadership is first and foremost about significantly enhancing revenue-generating opportunities—business development. As a thought leader, your firm is able to garner a disproportionate share of additional business, whether it's from prospects reaching out to you, existing clients, referrals from those clients, or working through referrals sources and intermediaries.

There are a multitude of internal advantages to being a thought leader as well. For example, a considerable advantage entails a superior ability to recruit and retain talent—the heart of a professional services firm. It also helps ensure that the professionals within the firm are at the cutting edge of their fields. While we clearly see these advantages, this book will concentrate on the ability to develop and distribute thought leadership products to garner additional revenues for the firm.

To be a thought leader as we define it, your firm not only has to be moving the field of specialization forward in various constructive ways, but it has to be well placed in the line of money. In effect, your professional services firm isn't a thought leader unless it is generating significantly disproportionate above-average returns because of its efforts. As a thought leader, your professional services firm will become renowned in desired circles that, in turn, appreciably contribute to a greatly expanded and quickening flow of money into the firm's bank account. It's about becoming eminent, then wealthy.

.

CHAPTER 5:
FAME, THEN FORTUNES

Thought leadership, from our perspective, is the product of two components—genius driving exceptional financial gain. Being brilliant without being profitable is very nice, but not all that meaningful if you're responsible for running a professional services firm. So many professionals hang their success, their careers, and the monetary well-being of themselves and their families, as well as their personal self-image, on their intellectual knowledge, agility and proficiencies. As we've noted, the problem for a great number of these professionals is that technical expertise—even at the highest levels—does not necessarily equate with money.

At the same time, we're fairly confident you're familiar with a wide swath of professional services firms that are doing quite well business-wise, even though you would not consider them to be very high-caliber. In fact, we're confident more than a handful of your competitors are clearly substandard, yet they seem to be doing fairly well. Clients and referral sources like them, and they try real hard. However, when it comes to delivering great (and sometimes even adequate) knowledge-based solutions, they tend to not make the grade. Still, many of these Incompetent Experts are probably regular competitors for the same clients your firm wants.

THE BOTTOM LINE
Thought leadership is all about becoming visible in a very positive way to decision-makers who are consequently more likely to engage your firm. Bluntly put, among certain circles—prospects, clients and referral sources—you want your firm to be famous. Moreover, at different levels, you want that fame to be tightly

linked with your expertise. As you're now backlit, you want to capitalize on the situation to generate new business.

In Exhibit 5.1, we have the bottom line algorithm. It's really very simple. We start with brilliance. That's the technical expertise embedded in the professionals within your firm, coupled with the outbound insights you advantageously uncover. You take all this intellectual capital, parse it, transform it, structure it and communicate it, resulting in your firm becoming a thought leader for particular audiences.

Now your firm is selectively famous. However, having your professional services firm known as one of the top authorities in a field is not enough—not at all. This level of recognition must enable the firm to create feasible and very attractive new business opportunities. Those opportunities—provided that you and the other managing partners at your firm can close and manage the engagements well—results in money to grow the firm, to share with employees, to give to loved ones, to enjoy yourself.

EXHIBIT 5.1: THE BOTTOM LINE ALGORITHM

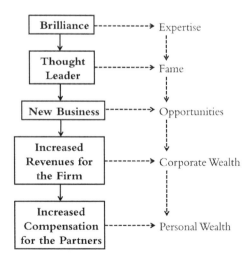

Looking at the big picture, thought leadership is about becoming selectively famous and then leveraging that status and profile to become wealthier. Thought leadership, when done very well, is one of the most sophisticated and sublime business development strategies existing today. More telling, it's one of the most effective and valuable business development strategies available to most professional services firms.

To be very transparent, thought leadership is a marketing strategy. By definition, all marketing strategies are about business development. And as a marketing strategy, thought leadership ties in tightly with the brand of the professional services firm. The complication is that in the world of professional services, high-potency branding is directed at two interconnected but distinct audiences, making becoming a thought leader all the more thorny and difficult—and all the more valuable.

THE POWER OF A DUAL-IMPACT BRAND

Take a moment to consider your professional services firm's branding. How would you, the other managing partners at your firm, your employees, your clients, your referral sources and even your competitors answer the following questions?

- What does your firm stand for?
- What are the core tenets of your firm's brand?
- How is your firm building and enhancing its brand?
- How is your firm benefiting from its brand?
- How are you measuring the value of your firm's brand?
- When it comes to branding, how can your firm improve?

We suspect that among the various groups we asked about, you'll get very little consistency. There have been times we've been surprised by a high degree of agreement, but those times are few and far between. Even when there is significant agreement, that doesn't mean the brand was in any way optimal or even on the right track.

To complicate the matter, a brand in the traditional sense is generally insufficient for most professional services firms. What's really required in today's ultra competitive world of professional services firms is a dual-impact brand.

Think for a moment about the audiences for your professional services firm's brand. It's more than highly probable that your firm has two very distinct audiences. One audience is composed of the people and companies (that is, clients and prospects) that can use and benefit from your firm's expertise. The other audience is composed of all the prospective referral sources. Your firm's brand needs to appeal to both of these audiences. This is only feasible when your firm actively seeks to create a dual-impact brand.

We just asked you to examine your professional services firm's brand from a number of vantage points. Take another few moments to consider the extent to which referral sources would associate your firm with each of the following propositions:
- An ability to enable them to make more money.
- A better understanding of various types of clienteles.
- Capable of providing state-of-the-art practice management insights and processes.
- An ability to deliver business development expertise that they can utilize.
- An education on how to more effectively source ideal clients.
- An understanding of how to help them better optimize their business models.

If at all possible, you want referral sources to strongly identify each of these attributes with your firm. This positioning is in addition to recognizing your firm as an authority in the services it provides clients.

There's no doubt that a professional services firm's dual-impact brand can be superlatively valuable in driving business to the firm. Being a thought leader is probably the most expeditious, effectual and dynamic way to build and strengthen a dual-impact brand. With your dual-impact brand, you have two interconnected messages (see Exhibit 5.2):

- You're telling prospects and clients that your professional services firm is replete with the experts they need to consult. The message is that the professionals within your firm are talented, possessing the skills and knowledge that can and will deliver the best solutions possible.

- You're telling referral sources that not only can your professional services firm do an exceptional job for their clients, it can also add substantial value to their business in one way or a variety of ways. In some respects, you're repeating your firm's message for clients. However, the firm's brand is also going beyond that in stating that it's a resource for referral sources who want to attain greater success.

EXHIBIT 5.2: THE DUAL-IMPACT BRAND

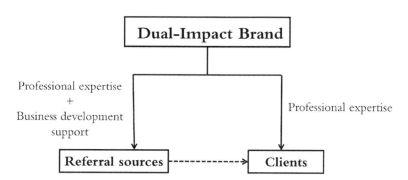

Thought leadership proves to be astounding in helping professional services firms create, nurture and capitalize on dual-impact brands. Becoming a thought leader isn't necessarily required, nor is it sufficient. A dual-impact brand is generally much more than being a thought leader. But this doesn't take away from the considerable expansion and improvements being a thought leader provides to a dual-impact brand.

THE CONNECTION BETWEEN THOUGHT LEADERSHIP AND A DUAL-IMPACT BRAND

For sourcing business from clients and referral sources, a professional services firm's powerful dual-impact brand can make a significant difference. While there are many ways to develop and strengthen a dual-impact brand, the most effectual and commanding way is by being a thought leader.

Your professional services firm's high-caliber dual-impact brand is its "fame." It creates positive and self-reinforcing recognition from prospects, clients, referral sources and ofttimes even competitors. There are a variety of ways to develop a high-caliber dual-impact brand, and you need to be cognizant of them all. Still, in the formula for creating and expanding an unassailable dual-impact brand, thought leadership can—and should—be a very potent independent variable. Thought leadership, done well, operating directly and as a cornerstone for a dual-impact brand, results in tremendous business development opportunities. There are, however, various levels of recognition as a thought leader that a professional services firm can garner. The highest level is to be a celebrity thought leader.

A CELEBRITY THOUGHT LEADER

As we consistently monitor various professional services firms, examining and periodically evaluating their thought leadership initiatives, we see a range of commitments to this marketing approach. Much of the efforts to become a thought leader or enhance such positioning are intermittent, if not erratic. This is often a function of fluctuating managerial will as well as structural and resource limitations. Even if thought leadership initiatives are intermittent, extensive business development benefits still accrue to the professional services firm.

Even when the thought leadership initiatives are restrained in scope, if done well, they can nonetheless be remarkably valuable ways for professional services firms to ratchet up their business development success, meaningfully generating new business opportunities and seriously boost revenues. At these times, professional services firms do indeed achieve a level of fame that translates into fortunes.

Take a few moments and think through the following two questions:

Question 1: What would happen if your professional services firm placed its thought leadership initiative at center stage?

Question 2: What would happen if your thought leadership efforts built a very loyal following of clients and referral sources?

As you're considering the implications of making becoming a thought leader central to your firm's business development efforts, it might be useful to consider two more questions.

Question 3: What would happen to your professional services firm's business development efforts if becoming a thought leader and maintaining that stature were the essence of its marketing strategy?

Question 4: If all this were the case, what would happen to the personal finances of professionals at the firm, including your own?

When a professional services firm makes a full-blown, all-out commitment to becoming a thought leader, the firm can go from being "industry famous" to being "industry eminent," transitioning from thought leader to celebrity thought leader (see Exhibit 5.3). If the thought leadership process is executed well and repeatedly, the firm will see continuous, explosive growth in sourcing new business.

EXHIBIT 5.3: FROM THOUGHT LEADER TO CELEBRITY THOUGHT LEADER

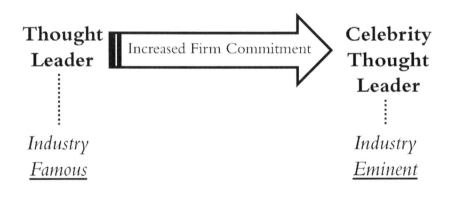

Thought Leader — Increased Firm Commitment → Celebrity Thought Leader

Industry Famous

Industry Eminent

Professional expertise

A VERY LOYAL FOLLOWING

When your professional services firm achieves celebrity stature, it has developed a very loyal following composed of clients and referral sources. At this point, your firm is providing a steady stream of intellectually predicated insights and actionable solutions, cleverly and skillfully chunked into products that it adroitly distributes. The thought leadership products are very much on point in enabling clients and referral sources to achieve greater ends. This very loyal following is quite willing, even happy, to pay in various ways for your firm's thought leadership products.

The thought leadership process detailed in *Part III: Becoming Profitably Brilliant* is the authoritative methodology that results in fame and, if more ardently pursued, celebrity, all while it results in more successful business development efforts.

While in some scenarios the desired audiences are both broad and deep, that tends to be the exception, not the norm. What's more common is that there are relatively limited but potentially highly profitable segments of a much larger audience that make sense for your firm. The critical objective is to build a deep and meaningful relationship with these segments so that they become very loyal followers. Let's clearly define the characteristics of this highly dependable cohort (see Exhibit 5.4):

- Your very loyal followers find the thought leadership products your firm develops to be very consequential and applicable in their businesses. In situation-specific ways, those products enrich them. Because of the value these followers derive, their loyalty remains with your firm as long as it continues to deliver both thought leadership products and its high-quality core services.

- Your very loyal followers are willing to pay quite well for the thought leadership products you provide. Payment can take a variety of forms. What currency they use to pay for thought leadership products depends on your business model (see *Chapter 9: Monetizing*).
- Your very loyal followers act as apostles for your firm's services and thought leadership products. Whether they're clients or referral sources, they are strong and persuasive advocates. Their actions are often instrumental in bringing new business to your firm.

EXHIBIT 5.4: CHARACTERISTICS OF VERY LOYAL FOLLOWERS

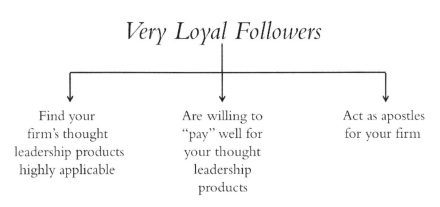

If having apostles is one objective of becoming a thought leader, a good starting point is to determine the baseline. Go through the following questions and see the extent to which your firm is garnering very loyal followers:

- Do your key clients invariably turn to your firm for additional or expanded services?
- Do your key clients actively and continually look to refer peerage to your firm?

- Are your key clients fairly indifferent to the cost of your services?
- Is your firm the first, if not the only, firm that important referral sources will recommend to their clients for the services your firm provides?
- Do important referral sources actively and continually look to introduce your firm to their clients?
- Do important referral sources intensely presell your firm to their clients?

If all your answers are "yes," then you have apostles. If not, becoming a celebrity thought leader can do a great deal to help your professional services firm get there.

It's very possible to profit handsomely from becoming a thought leader by intermittently developing high-quality thought leadership products. On the other hand, a professional services firm wanting to be a celebrity thought leader must make a considerable commitment to developing and delivering high-quality thought leadership products with a fair degree of consistency.

COMMITTING TO SUCCESS

To become a celebrity thought leader, a professional services firm should look at the endeavor as a campaign as opposed to a one-off assault or even a series of discrete initiatives. A viable thought leadership campaign is optimally an extended discourse between the professional services firm and its desired target audiences of prospects, clients and referral sources.

You want these audiences to recognize the knowledge, capabilities, value and value-added services your firm brings to them. This usually takes some time and repeated exposure predicated on new thought leadership products. By looking at thought leadership as a campaign, your firm is intensely creating and burnishing its brand—preferably its dual-impact brand.

While a single thought leadership initiative can, and usually does, result in considerable new business, it is noticeably more limited compared to a campaign. Meanwhile, the business boost from a well-executed thought leadership initiative can provide—and often does provide—the springboard to a broader and more involved campaign.

Becoming a celebrity thought leader requires a commitment of resources. The managing partners of the professional services firm, for example, must be solidly behind the effort (see *Chapter 7: Strategizing*). This usually entails working closely with the individuals responsible for developing the thought leadership products, connecting with audience segments (see *Chapter 8: Productizing*) and ensuring there's appropriate follow-up (see *Chapter 9: Monetizing*).

Becoming a celebrity thought leader can get expensive. It's crucial to determine whether your professional services firm is able and willing to make the necessary investment to grow geo-exponentially. The costs range widely based on a slew of factors, such as the use of research technologies and the depth and breadth of the distribution strategy. Because of the expenses involved, some professional services firms team up to share in the glow and financial returns of becoming industry celebrities (see *Chapter 7: Strategizing* and *Coda: The Future of Profitable Brilliance*).

As we've discussed, being profitably brilliant is the essence, the result of being a thought leader or, better yet, a celebrity thought leader. While the transformative process from Hidden Talent to Talented Expert—and beyond—is quite mechanical and straightforward, with often boringly reliable results, elements of cleverness, ingenuity, originality and even high cunning can be central to becoming a celebrity thought leader commanding a relatively small but very powerful army of very loyal followers. It's at this point that your professional services firm has bridged the gap from thought leader to celebrity thought leader.

For almost all professional services firms, being a thought leader is the preferred option. It's even more preferable for a professional services firm to become a celebrity thought leader. It's hard to find managing partners at professional services firms who don't want their firm to be highly recognized as one of the very top, if not the top, expert for their firm's offerings. While the logic for professional services firms to strive to become thought leaders is especially solid, there are potential adverse repercussions when it is done badly.

THOUGHT LEADERSHIP DONE BADLY

Becoming a thought leader will bring scores of benefits to most any professional services firm—but there's a downside if the firm gets it wrong. That downside can prove quite painful, if not brutal. Basically, there are three categories in which professional services firms can find themselves when thought leadership initiatives are done badly (see Exhibit 5.5):

- *Invisibles.* The best-case scenario of doing a poor job at becoming a thought leader is that the professional services firm experiences no repercussions from its prospects, clients and referral sources. In these circumstances, all the time spent, effort expended and monies invested are just written off. However, when a professional services firm executes a thought leadership initiative badly, the best-case scenario is not always what happens.

- **Benchwarmers.** When thought leadership efforts falter, the consequences can be the adverse of what was intended. Instead of being seen as a Talented Expert, the professional services firm conveys that its understanding of critical industry issues is superficial at best or its solutions are anything but. A badly conceived or executed thought leadership initiative can easily convey that the professional services firm belongs in the minor leagues, warming the bench or more likely carrying the water, as opposed to playing on the all-star team.

- **Radioactives.** What's even more detrimental is the "reverse halo" effect, where its poor attempt at becoming a thought leader actually diminishes the professional services firm's offerings in the eyes of prospects, clients and referral sources. In effect, not only does the firm not achieve the status of a Talented Expert, but it brings its reputation for high-caliber expertise down a notch or two or more. It's a worse fate than being a Hidden Talent.

EXHIBIT 5.5: THOUGHT LEADERSHIP DONE BADLY

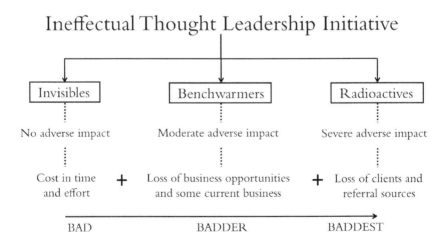

These possible adverse consequences don't mean a professional services firm should abandon the idea of becoming a thought leader. What it does mean is that your professional services firm should approach the project judiciously and prudently. The decision to become a thought leader must be made very carefully and methodically. The managing partners need to think through what they want to accomplish and how becoming a leading industry authority will actualize these goals.

Becoming a thought leader is a proven way to transform a professional services firm for the better by creating and filling a pipeline of new exceptional clients. It's also instrumental in cementing and expanding relationships with current clients. So if a professional services firm chooses to go in this direction, it's essential to ensure that the managing partners are willing to put in the time, effort and resources to do it well (see *Chapter 7: Strategizing*).

FOOD FOR THOUGHT

A dual-impact brand powered by thought leadership could readily enable a professional services firm to become industry-eminent—a celebrity thought leader—and garner all the rewards bestowed on the famous and talented. A cadre of very loyal followers translates into a near-unending pipeline of high-caliber prospects for your firm's services. Just think about what this could mean for your professional services firm as well as the personal finances of the partners.

What you always have to keep at the top of your mind is that thought leadership is not an act of altruism—quite the opposite, in fact: *Thought leadership is soundly about business development.*

Those very loyal followers can be, for many professional services firms, a rock-solid financial foundation and then some.

Pecuniary success is only possible when the professional services firm is staunchly behind any endeavor of the firm to become a thought leader. The managing partners have to seriously believe in the advantages to the firm of becoming a thought leader and, better yet, a celebrity thought leader. Moreover, this commitment has to be supported in action. Keep in mind that half-hearted attempts can sometimes be counterproductive.

INTERLUDE: A REPUTATION FOR CEO RESEARCH

LESLIE GAINES-ROSS, CHIEF REPUTATION STRATEGIST, WEBER SHANDWICK

Ask Google if Dr. Leslie Gaines-Ross is a thought leader. Google seems to think so. She comes to the top of the listings when searching for "CEO Reputation." In fact, she takes up the whole first page. Leslie owns the category to herself and by extension so does the global PR and communication strategy firm she works for, Weber Shandwick. And why not, she literally and figuratively wrote the book on the subject. Fascinated by how a CEO's reputation impacts business outcomes, Leslie broke ground on the topic. When she realized that there was little research on the value of a good CEO reputation, she just did it herself. Armed with data showing that 50% of a company's reputation can be attributed to the CEO's reputation, she wrote her first book in 2003 entitled, not surprisingly, *CEO Capital: A Guide to Building CEO Reputation and Company Success.* The book positioned her and the agency she worked for at the time as a leader in helping CEOs build better reputations on behalf of their companies from the first 100 days to the last 100 hours. As importantly, her thought leadership elevated the reputation of the firm she worked for then, the PR industry in general and has made Weber Shandwick the go-to firm on CEO and corporate reputation.

Leslie's interest in CEO reputation and its link to business success started at an early age. She grew up the daughter of a successful businessman and entrepreneur who, along with his brother-in-law, founded the Atlantic Wire & Cable company and built it from scratch into a thriving business. She recalls having regular discussions around the kitchen table initiated by her father about business and particularly about the people in charge of those businesses. Her father believed that he could apply valuable lessons from the best practices of CEOs of the world's biggest companies—AT&T, IBM and GM—while reading about them in his favorite business magazine. While business was always a topic of conversation in her household, her interest in what drives positive and negative perceptions about companies started when her father's business foundered, finding itself on the wrong end of creditors and lawyers. The concept of how "reputation" can be built over a lifetime and destroyed in what seemed like moments was an all-too-real dilemma for her and her family to deal with. And though her father's business and his reputation would recover stronger than ever, she never forgot the lessons learned and became forever fascinated with how leadership can make a difference. She did not inherit her father's love of building a family business per se, but rather developed a personal passion for understanding why and how businesses succeed or fail as a result of the reputation of the person at the top.

Like many other successful thought leaders, Leslie came to her position through a confluence of events that led her to a moment of insight. While working as the marketing and communications director at Fortune magazine, she became enamored with its Most Admired Companies rankings. She decided that this consuming interest might hold the keys to her life's work. Suddenly, her academic training, family upbringing and life-long interest in reputation came together. This discovery still remains with her and she has tirelessly spearheaded thought leadership on the reputation management, ranging from CEO reputation, corporate reputation, reputation warfare, executive reputation, online reputation, and reputation recovery.

Now as Weber Shandwick's Chief Reputation Strategist, Leslie continues to focus on the ever- changing world of reputation. Her second book has been published, *Corporate Reputation: 12 Steps to Safeguarding and Recovering Reputation* (2008, John Wiley & Sons, www.corporatereputation12steps.com) which describes how companies can now restore their tarnished names. Her favorite reputation quote is from Warren Buffett: "If you lose dollars for the firm by bad decisions, I will be understanding. If you lose reputation for the firm, I will be ruthless." As Leslie says: "Amen."

PART III: BECOMING PROFITABLY BRILLIANT

CHAPTER 6:
THE THOUGHT LEADERSHIP PROCESS

We've presented the logic and rationale for professional services firms of becoming thought leaders. We recommend that you spend some time determining how being a thought leader could be transformative for your firm. You can review the questions we raised in *Chapter 4: The Case for Thought Leadership*. After you've reconsidered these questions, how would you answer the following ones?

- How would your professional services firm benefit from having a powerful dual-impact brand?
- What would happen if your firm had a sizable and highly motivated cohort of very loyal followers?
- What obstacles does your firm face to becoming a thought leader?
- What obstacles does your firm face to becoming a celebrity thought leader?

We've found that the last two questions are the most difficult ones for many managing partners to answer. We often hear managing partners reel off a litany of reasons for not devoting the requisite resources to becoming a thought leader. Some of the more common ones are:

"We're as smart as or smarter than anyone else. Why do we need to bother with becoming a thought leader?"
"We're too busy prospecting to work on becoming a thought leader."

"We have better uses for our marketing dollars."

"We are thought leaders. Our clients just don't know it."

In our experience, cutting through all the excuses, one of the most common and misinformed reasons for not becoming a thought leader is that the managing partners actually don't know how to do so. While they generally understand many of the elements required, putting them all together, as well as actualizing the process and deriving synergies and maximum results, is more than a little daunting.

THE PHASES OF THE THOUGHT LEADERSHIP PROCESS

What you need to understand is that the thought leadership process is actually fairly mechanical. In Exhibit 6.1, we see the thought leadership process.

It starts with an overarching strategy with clear goals and objectives—including financial goals and strategic objectives. Then we turn to creating thought leadership products. This is where the intellectual capital is distilled from a conglomeration of ideas, concepts and possibilities. That capital is subsequently transformed into thought leadership content, and in turn packaged into thought leadership products and communicated to target audiences. Subsequently, the professionals at the firm adroitly follow up, resulting in new profitable engagements.

EXHIBIT 6.1: THE THOUGHT LEADERSHIP PROCESS

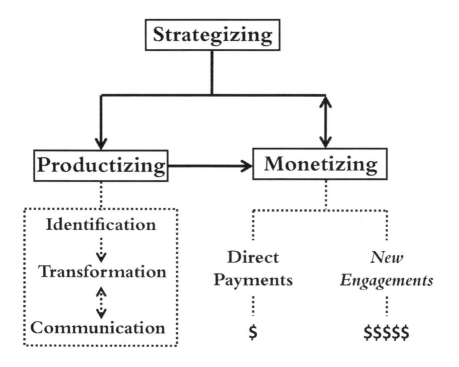

We continue to emphasize:

Successful thought leadership is not about ego gratification or altruism. Successful thought leadership is all about generating new business.

Success due to thought leadership is about greater financial achievements for the professional services firm. Furthermore, from our perspective, we can easily conclude that the greater success of the firm translates into greater personal wealth for the professionals involved.

Let's briefly consider each of the phases in the thought leadership process.

Strategizing is the phase of the process that permeates every other. This is when you develop the blueprint for your professional services firm's thought leadership initiative. The objective is to carefully and critically think through the other phases and steps in the process and develop an overarching game plan. Furthermore, you constantly need to readjust the thought leadership initiative. The more you vigilantly consider, delineate and continually refine the various components of the initiative, the more likely is that your firm will connect with desirable high-caliber prospects and excel, and the more likely that professionals therein will personally profit.

Productizing is where the intellectual capital is first discerned and then transformed into thought leadership content. It's then taken a step further and packaged into readily consumable forms—thought leadership products. There are a set number of possible thought leadership products. Which ones to pursue and how precisely to package the thought leadership content is a function of the interplay of available resources and capabilities, the underlying nature of the intellectual capital and the characteristics of the target audiences. Moreover, the way your professional services firm communicates with the desired audience is built into the thought leadership products.

Monetizing refers to the professional services firm's ability to generate revenues from the benefits and advantages accrued by the thought leadership products. The thought leadership products enable your firm to start building rapport with a large number of high-value audience members. Then, through an integrative self-selection progression, a percentage of these audience members decide to do business with you. This is something you have to be very attuned to and focused on. In effect, you need to always be asking: "How does the thought leadership initiative enable my firm to profit?" While the bottom line is an increase in your bottom line, there are usually a number of intermediary goals along the way. Tracking these intermediary goals is often instrumental to getting the financial results you're looking for.

WHAT WORKS BEST

Some professional services firms engage in thought leadership initiatives as opposed to more expansive campaigns. Some firms meticulously and intensely go through the entire process we've just presented with the aim of becoming solidly defined as celebrity thought leaders. Some firms take a much more à la carte approach. For example, they might conduct an insightful and intensive empirical study, and make selective and targeted use of the report they produce.

What's most telling is that all these professional services firms, approaching their own thought leadership initiatives in their own way, get to the same place—greater business development success—to a varying degree. It's very plain that for professional services firms, providing valuable thought leadership products to target audiences, coupled with the proper follow-up, can regularly result in attractive new engagements. The benefits amassing to the professional services firm vary based on the extent to which these efforts enhance its thought leadership prominence.

We've worked with professional services firms to create comprehensive thought leadership campaigns, and we've worked with firms to develop specific thought leadership initiatives. We've also worked with professional services firms to address specific components of the thought leadership process. In all these cases, the professional services firms benefited as they intended.

What's also very important is that in all these cases, the agenda of the respective firms took precedent.

The best way for a professional services firm to go—campaign or initiative or components—is predicated on its capabilities, its goals and objectives, and its current branding. What needs to be readily understood is that there isn't a best solution, as one size fits no one. What you and your partners need to do is understand the machinery of the thought leadership process, so you can make erudite decisions as to how your professional services firm can attain the greatest benefits accruing to thought leaders within your firm's operational parameters.

RUNNING THE NUMBERS

The essence of being in the line of money is taking action that you stoutly trust will make your firm, and consequently you, more successful and therefore wealthier. Ensuring that you are in the line of money proves essential to joining the ranks of the self-made super-rich (see *Appendix A: Money Rules*). Moreover, it's equally essential in all endeavors where your ultimate goal is greater achievement and ensuing wealth.

Having just accentuated the need to customize the approach your professional services firm takes to becoming a thought leader, it's crucial that you understand the financial implications—costs and projected returns over realistic time frames. In essence, it can be very helpful to construct a pro forma for your firm's thought leadership efforts.

While we refer to this approach as running the numbers, what you're dealing with are not only the financial status and implications but the strategic ones as well. There will be times when nonmonetary considerations overshadow strictly financial ones. What's important is to clearly understand all the projected consequences—good, bad and shades of gray. This will best enable you and your partners to make well-reasoned decisions.

When done well, the very operation of running the numbers provides enormously valuable insights and perspectives. It often produces a set of prompts and questions that can motivate you and your partners to openly and blatantly address an array of issues that usually extend beyond thought leadership considerations to multiple facets of the firm's business model.

The understandings you can derive by astutely working through projected financials, buttressed by strategic calculations, will enable you to make superior decisions all along the way. When it comes to becoming a thought leader, we also advocate that in running the numbers you go deep into your organization's framework and business model to understand and tweak the expected and probable consequences of thought leadership initiatives on the overall firm, as well as the impacted professionals within the firm (including yourself).

FOOD FOR THOUGHT

There's no magic, none at all. The thought leadership process, at its finest, is quite nuanced, but it's far from proprietary or secret. The advantage we have is that we're very experienced at helping professional services firms as well as individual professionals become thought leaders and celebrity thought leaders. Our decades of in-the-field experimentation and practice translate into an internalized understanding of the best practices in this specialty. It's not very different from the business expertise of any professional who has a concrete grasp of the technical material and has seen more than enough real-life situations to know how best to deal with diverse client situations.

In detailing the thought leadership process, we recognize that quite a few managing partners at professional services firms can readily refine their efforts or fairly easily draw up and implement a very effective thought leadership initiative. The intellectual abilities and fortitude captured in many professional services firms can be adroitly applied to crafting and implementing state-of-the-art thought leadership initiatives and campaigns.

CHAPTER 7:
STRATEGIZING

Having run the numbers (see *Chapter 6: The Thought Leadership Process*) and made the decision to become a thought leader, the first phase of the process is strategizing. Here you and your partners develop the game plan for your professional services firm's thought leadership initiative. The intent is to carefully map out all the components of the initiative, along with the desired outcomes.

We've found that more than a few professional services firms get wrapped up in crafting the strategy, to the detriment of actually becoming a thought leader. On occasion, some firms never get beyond this phase. The strategy dies a slow death from protracted meetings and from the myriad ways some partners can avoid doing almost anything where there's accountability attached. We've seen professional services firms do an outstanding job of thinking through the issues over and over again, never taking action. Let's remember that strategizing is only the start of a thought leadership initiative.

A number of perspectives need to be addressed as part of this phase. Some of the key components include:
- A high level of managing partner support.
- Defining success.
- Leveraging the brand.
- Determining appropriate domain expertise.
- Understanding the target audiences.
- Competitor analysis.
- Dedicating resources.
- Refining.

Let's now consider each of these components in greater detail.

A HIGH LEVEL OF MANAGING PARTNER SUPPORT

Unless the managing partners of your professional services firm are seriously committed to their firm becoming a thought leader, it's not going to happen. What's more, without champions at the firm, it's just about impossible to develop and implement an effective thought leadership initiative. The champions are essential to navigate the multitude of political land mines and to make sure the commitment to becoming a thought leader continues when the inevitable glitches occur.

At the very least, there has to be a managing partner who recognizes the value of being a thought leader and is able to deal with the often political and ego-derived machinations at the firm. Some of the other qualities of an exceptional champion include:

- An understanding of business development.
- An ability to address new situations with an open mind.
- A strong commitment to the success of the professional services firm.
- An ability to work with as well as manage other high-caliber, sometimes touchy professionals.
- A strong work ethic.

The greater the managing partners' level of commitment to becoming a thought leader, the more likely the firm will garner the multiple benefits therein. Consider the following questions in ascertaining the level of managing partner commitment:

- Do the managing partners seriously want their firm to be a thought leader?
- Do the managing partners seriously want their firm to be a celebrity thought leader?

- Are there one or more champions for each thought leadership initiative?
- Are the managing partners willing to wholeheartedly make an initial commitment to the firm's becoming a thought leader?
- Can the managing partners identify some of the benefits of being a thought leader?

The more "yes" answers, the better.

It's not uncommon for managing partners to learn to appreciate the advantages of being a thought leader as well as recognize the effort it takes to get there. We've found that in some professional services firms, business development successes translate into greater commitments from the managing partners. A lot of this has to do with the need to prove the value of a thought leadership initiative. Keep in mind that a great many professionals equate technical expertise with business success (see *Chapter 2: Hidden Talents or Talented Experts*).

DEFINING SUCCESS

It's often best to begin with the end in mind. If your professional services firm is going to commit the array of requisite resources required to become a thought leader, what should the results of the endeavor be? In working with professional services firms in setting goals, we find it's usually best to derive and specify:

- *The financial end goal.* This goal is the one that makes becoming a thought leader truly worthwhile. What revenues are the managing partners looking to generate from being a thought leader? This is regularly a function of the firm's strategic objectives and capabilities, coupled with its business model. By running the numbers (see *Chapter 6: The*

Thought Leadership Process), you're most likely to develop a lucid and on-point understanding of the financial benefits of your firm's thought leadership initiative.

- **The strategic end goals.** From competitive positioning to talent management, the managing partners are interested in achieving certain strategic objectives. Some of these goals may support the financial end goal. It's equally important to carefully delineate all the nonfinancial objectives.

- **Intermediary goals.** These are the nonfinancial metrics your professional services firm can employ to measure success. Usually, but not exclusively, they're the business development goals your firm has specified. This is very much a numbers game. Therefore, your awareness of the ability and rates of the professionals within your firm in closing high-caliber prospects is quite useful.

Operationally, it's best to define your firm's financial and strategic goals first. Then it becomes pretty straightforward to determine the intermediary goals your firm needs to achieve to reach its financial end goal. Tied to the intermediary goals and your firm's definitions of success are time frames. Becoming a thought leader takes times. Becoming a celebrity thought leader takes incrementally more time. In specifying success, it's essential to do so within realistic chronological parameters.

With respect to time frames, it's crucial to be cognizant of the tipping points. Following a few years of efforts, for example, your firm may suddenly become a thought leader. Depending on your firm's intentions, it will take some time to achieve the sought-after recognition. While there will be meaningful benefits along the way (see *Chapter 3: What Is a Thought Leader?* and *Chapter 4: The Case for Thought Leadership*), quite often at a certain point—the tipping point—all the puzzle pieces come together, and the professional services firm takes an exponential leap in stature. Then, with a persistent flow of exceptional thought leadership products, combined with religiously executed follow-up, the professional services firm reaches another tipping point, becoming a celebrity thought leader (see Exhibit 7.1). Along the way, your firm is achieving greater business development success, and the growth rate of this success continues to accelerate.

EXHIBIT 7.1: TWO TIPPING POINTS

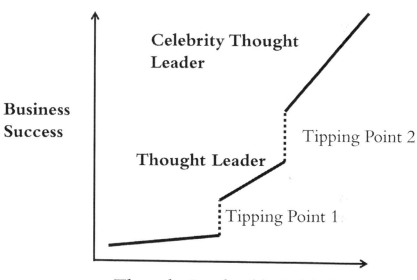

LEVERAGE THE BRAND

Many professional services firms have a brand that has evolved over time. If your firm has a brand, and the decision is that it remains appropriate and viable, then it's beneficial to take advantage of your firm's brand in constructing thought leadership initiatives. Going through the following steps can help you think about where you can leverage your firm's brand.

Step 1: Specify the core tenets of your professional services firm's brand.

Step 2: Identify the target audiences for your firm's brand. Included here is how your firm wants prospects, clients and referral sources to relate to the brand.

Step 3: Detail the communication strategies being employed to reach the target audiences. It's often quite useful to gauge the viability and effectiveness of each strategy.

Step 4: Determine the overlap between your firm's current core tenets, target audiences and communication strategies, and where being a thought leader will garner the greatest benefits. This then commonly becomes a decision about whether to fill in where there's weakness or plow ahead where there's strength.

Step 5: Capitalize on the overlap and/or the untapped potential. This is a function of the decision the managing partners made in Step 4. Even when the choice is to build a dual-impact brand where brand equity doesn't currently exist, there are usually still great opportunities to leverage key core tenets of the firm's brand.

The greater the overlap, the more your firm will be able to become a thought leader on the foundation of an already established brand. However, even if there isn't a great deal of overlap or if the thought leadership initiative is intended to bolster a specialization in the firm that does not tightly connect to the brand, there are still benefits to derive from a solid brand. It's just going to require a little more creativity to capitalize on it.

DETERMINING APPROPRIATE DOMAIN EXPERTISE

Most professional services firms provide a range of services. A law firm, for instance, can have attorneys who deal with corporate matters, intellectual property, real estate and so forth. Most professional services firms are adept at working with a number of different types of clients. An accounting firm might have specializations in broker-dealers, nursing homes, production companies and so on.

It's often advantageous, if not a requisite, for the managing partners of the professional services firm to proactively decide just where they want to position the firm as a thought leader. If we presume that a professional services firm is, by and large, a Hidden Talent abounding with Savants, and the firm has multiple specialties, then decisions really do need to be made as to which specialties—and which professionals—should be backlit. The following questions can be helpful in making this decision:

- What are the highest-level types of technical expertise embedded in your firm?
- What specializations are strategically important to your firm?
- What specializations generate the most revenues?
- What specializations generate the most profits?
- Which clienteles or desired clienteles does your firm want to cultivate for strategic and financial reasons?
- What referral sources does your firm want to cultivate for strategic and financial reasons?

In working with professional services firms, we've sometimes taken these questions and pushed hard to make sure the managing partners were clear as to where they wanted to become thought leaders. However, we've found that for many profes-sional services firms, most of the time it's pretty self-evident where the appropriate domain expertise lies.

While we talk about the professional services firm being a thought leader, and possibly a celebrity thought leader, we're usually referring to a particular group or unit within the firm that possesses specific domain expertise. So a wealth manage-ment firm might be a thought leader when it comes to the needs, wants and preferences of owners of small and midsize businesses, but that doesn't mean it's a thought leader when it comes to hedge fund management companies and their owners.

Most of the time thought leadership is very domain expertise specific. Now, it's certainly possible to define the area of domain expertise quite broadly. At the same time, it's quite possible for a professional services firm to be a thought leader in multiple areas of domain expertise. What's required is that the managing partners look at these as business decisions and run the num-bers (see *Chapter 6: The Thought Leadership Process*).

IDENTIFYING THE TARGET AUDIENCES

Understanding—really understanding—who the audience is for any thought leadership initiative is critical. It's extremely impor-tant that clients, prospects and referral sources know that your professional services firm is an expert in specific areas. This way, you're directing your efforts to the people and companies—the decision-makers—that can enable your firm to be more prosper-ous. While it might be heartwarming that family, friends, and coworkers know your firm is expert that rarely, if ever, directly translates into money.

With a focus clearly on prospects, clients and referral sources, it's usually important to get as appropriately incremental as possible. There are a number of ways to accomplish this. The following are two often-employed methodologies:

- *Concentrate on ideal clients and referral sources.* You determine these ideal clients based on a critical evaluation of your current best clients and referral sources matched against the firm's business goals and objectives. The closer the professionals at your firm are to these ideal clients and referral sources, the better they'll be able to provide ideas and perspectives for the next steps (see *Chapter 8: Productizing*).

- *Conduct a taxonomical assessment of desired clients and referral sources.* The aim here is to sequentially and systematically narrow down the larger universe of prospective clients and referral sources to very specific desired types. This winnowing-out process is tied in closely with the projected returns your professional services firm can garner by focusing on the smallest, most refined but fiscally appropriate segments.

Once the managing partners of a professional services firm have identified the types of clients and referral sources they believe are worth the effort to become a thought leader, it's often wise to run the possibilities through one more crucial filter. At this point, it's generally beneficial to run the numbers again and then some.

For many professional services firms, what's essential to realize is that being a thought leader is commonly target audience specific. It's less common for the professional services firm to be the thought leader with respect to process as opposed to client-centered content.

In many situations, the target audiences for thought leadership products are self-evident. However, when this isn't the case, putting in the time and effort to make certain your firm is targeting the best audiences is very worthwhile.

COMPETITOR ANALYSIS

Becoming a thought leader is a powerfully pervasive approach to marketing and one that's likely to only escalate in appeal as competition increases, clients become choosier as well as more cost-sensitive, reaching motivated prospects continues to get more difficult and so forth (see *Coda: The Future of Profitable Brilliance*).

With more and more professional services firms entering the fray to become thought leaders, a relatively small number will attain meaningful success. And only a relatively small percentage of those firms that are successful will attain the stature of a celebrity thought leader. Along the same lines, while many professional services firms have a brand, comparatively few have a powerful dual-impact brand. To significantly increase your firm's chances of being successful, it's highly advantageous to be attuned to what your competitors are doing in this arena and how they're doing it. The following exercise can be helpful in this regard.

Step 1: Identify five to ten other firms that the managing partners at your firm agree are key competitors for particular services to select target audiences.

Step 2: On a scale of one (not doing anything) to ten (extremely active), specify the extent to which each of these firms is striving to become a thought leader with respect to the identified domain expertise.

Step 3: For those firms rated seven or higher, detail what they're doing to become thought leaders or increase their ranking as thought leaders. Make sure to provide very specific examples of their thought leadership products.

Step 4: In your estimation, specify how successful their thought leadership initiatives are. Detail how their target audiences are responding, including what they're doing well and where they're missing the mark.

Step 5: Identify the approaches, mechanisms and resources these firms are employing to either become thought leaders or maintain their positioning.

Understanding what competitors are doing to become thought leaders, in conjunction with your firm's experience of their high-caliber prospects and clients, allows the managing partners at your firm to make strategic decisions concerning thought leadership content and products. There are a number of strategic ways to differentiate a professional services firm in this regard, such as (see Exhibit 7.2):

- *The step strategy.* The professional services firm works off the thought leadership content (not the precise products) of competitors. The solution set is an incremental but meaningful improvement on what is currently available. The following are the principle versions of this strategy:
  - o Giant step is a large improvement over what a competitor is doing, using similar thought leadership content.
  - o Step up is a minor but noticeable improvement over what a competitor is doing.
  - o Side step is when your firm develops a close variant of a competitor's thought leadership products, with a few twists.
  - o Back step is where your firm enhances the core elements of a competitor's thought leadership initiative.

- *The superiority strategy.* The professional services firm goes head-to-head with competitors based on the same or very similar thought leadership content. The goal is to deliver a considerably better set of solutions and/or a superior experience. The winner is the professional services firm that is able to execute better.

- *The innovation strategy.* The professional services firm chooses to avoid any conflicts or perceptual positioning overlaps, and develops thought leadership content that is new and consequently extremely applicable and appealing to prospects, clients and referral sources. There are a number of variations of this strategy, including:

  o Fast response, when the professional services firm addresses topical and situational issues and concerns.

  o Deep dive, where your firm extensively dissects an audience of professional services, developing original, leveraged creative or surprisingly clever thought leadership products.

  o Cross-disciplines have your firm drawing from other non-aligned fields to develop thought leadership products.

EXHIBIT 7.2: COMPETITOR DIFFERENTIATION

Strategies

Step	Superiority	Innovation
Incremental advantages	Head-to-head, but better	New creative and/or clever thought leadership products

An evaluation of what competitors are doing with respect to thought leadership could be very useful. However, it's constructive to keep in mind that it's a very big world, and adroit exploitation of time can be a strategic tool in this environment.

DEDICATING RESOURCES

Becoming a thought leader, let alone a celebrity thought leader, can be a costly endeavor. The combination of committed professional time, including managing partner commitment, coupled with direct costs and indirect opportunity costs, can really add up. What's more, as thought leadership is becoming a critical battleground for professional services firms (see *Coda: The Future of Profitable Brilliance*), it's foolish, if not out-and-out counterproductive, to try to cut corners (see *Chapter 5: Fame, Then Fortunes*).

You need to determine what resources your firm will need to devote to reach the designated intermediate goals as well as the strategic goals and financial end goal. While there are a number of ways to accomplish this, one of the most basic is creating a fundamental project grid. The grid should include activities, resource requirements and costs. It should also incorporate the degree to which particular resources are available within your firm. In this regard, you need to conduct an in-depth inventory of relevant capabilities. The only major addition might be designating the results or deliverables tied closely to the activities. It's often useful to segment the project grid by the phases of the thought leadership process.

Central to allocating resources is running the numbers (see *Chapter 6: The Thought Leadership Process*). In this capacity, some professional services firms run the numbers under a wide range of scenarios. While looking at a handful of scenarios usually makes sense, we advise working through the most probable scenarios.

We've found two very critical sets of decisions that the managing partners at professional services firms need to make when they discuss resource allocations. They are:

- The use of internal resources (that is, inside the firm) as opposed to external resources (that is, from providers).
- Teaming up with another firm or organization for strategic reasons as well as cost mitigation.

Let's take a closer look at each of these sets of decisions.

In-house versus outsourced. With thought leadership initiatives, there are major trade-offs between doing the work within your firm and using outside professionals. Very often professional services firms experiment and quickly strike a balance between developing thought leadership initiatives on their own and bringing in outside specialists. Here's an effective way for many professional services firms to decide on the loci of elements in a thought leadership initiative:

Step 1: Turning to the project grid for a thought leadership initiative, identify if the expertise is or is not available in-house. This is strictly a binary assessment.

Step 2: For those resource requirements that are available in-house, using a one (limited proficiency) to ten (complete proficiency) scale, rate the ability of the in-house resources to effectively perform the function. For those resource requirements rated seven or higher, your firm should consider doing the work in-house. With respect to the resource requirements rated five and six, a quick cost-benefit analysis is probably a good move. For those resources rated four or less, you should consider outsourcing or bringing the respective abilities in-house.

Step 3: For those resources for which your firm is considering employing outside providers, define the metrics you'll use to evaluate their deliverables. Then monitor these deliverables against the preset metrics. This will enable you to more accurately use and manage such providers going forward.

With thought leadership increasingly becoming a key competitive battleground for professional services firms, a growing number of providers are seeking to assist professional services firms (see *Coda: The Future of Profitable Brilliance*). Consequently, you'll need to consider a number of criteria in selecting outside providers, including (see Exhibit 7.3):

- *Integrity.* In every professional relationship, the integrity of all the parties is critical. Every professional must have confidence in the veracity and reliability of the selected provider.
- *Process expertise.* Demonstrable expertise at implementing the thought leadership process is key. To the extent that selected components of the thought leadership process are sought, the provider needs to be able to show relevant proficiency.
- *Track record.* Experience at helping professional services firms or even professionals become thought leaders as well as celebrity thought leaders is crucial. A history of accomplishments goes a long way toward validating the knowledge and abilities of a provider.
- *Consultative.* An ability to work adeptly and smoothly with other professionals is quite important. As management and other professionals at your firm will be intimately involved in developing and promoting the firm's thought leadership products, the provider must be able to work

cooperatively with very smart, motivated and sometimes difficult professionals.

- **Domain expertise.** Specific knowledge, capabilities and insights concerning or in demand by the target audiences play a role. Such comprehension and proficiencies can expedite the development of on-point thought leadership initiatives. However, of all the criteria, this is the least important, as your firm has the requisite knowledge and insights, which usually just need to be brought forth.

EXHIBIT 7.3: CRITERIA FOR OUTSOURCED PROVIDER

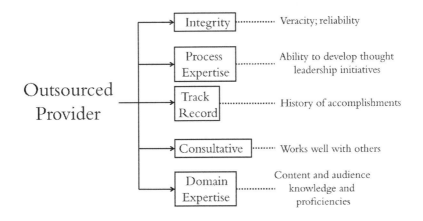

Teaming up. As noted, becoming a thought leader can be a potentially expensive endeavor, relatively speaking. If you see the benefits to your professional services firm in becoming a thought leader but are daunted by the costs and proficiencies it requires, there's always the option of teaming up.

By teaming up, we're not talking about employing outside providers. Instead, we're usually talking about joint ventures with another professional services firm. This cooperative approach is gaining traction. We're seeing an increasing number of non-competing professional services firms working agreeably in tandem to become thought leaders.

Depending on your firm's objectives and budget, teaming up can be quite practicable. It's important to ensure that by teaming up you are maximizing the opportunity for the professionals at your firm—and potentially yourself (see *Appendix A: Money Rules*).

To make this really work, you need to be very clear about what your professional services firm is bringing to the venture and what the other professional services firm or other type of organization is bringing. You have to go into the endeavor knowing the division of labor and costs between the two (or more) firms. You should also be explicit about the strategic value each party has and how to share this. Some of the questions to consider include the following:

- How can each professional services firm benefit from the brand of the other?
- What distribution capabilities does each firm possess?
- What capabilities does each firm have concerning the development of intellectual capital?
- How can both firms work cooperatively to convert the intellectual capital into thought leadership content and then into thought leadership products?
- What other resources can each professional services firm contribute to the undertaking?

As with any joint venture, you will need to be attentive to a number of issues, such as:

- The crediting of the intellectual capital, thought leadership content and thought leadership products, which is tied to the way you can make it part of your firm's dual-impact brand.

- The ownership of the intellectual capital, thought leadership content and thought leadership products.
- The limitations on the use of the thought leadership products, including the audiences with which each firm can use them.
- The ability to upgrade the thought leadership products independently or with different joint venture partners.

The more valuable the thought leadership products are, the more likely—if there's conflict—that there will be a messy divorce among the firms that teamed up. We therefore recommend that if you do decide to team up to develop and implement a thought leadership initiative, you set out the divorce proceedings in advance.

REFINING THE THOUGHT LEADERSHIP INITIATIVE

While it would be fantastic to put a thought leadership initiative together and then implement it, the reality is that a lot of adjustments are required as projections and intentions confront reality. You'll need to constantly reevaluate the elements of the thought leadership initiative and make modifications to achieve the desired results. The extent of the needed modifications can range from very minor to quite involved.

Essential to the success of any thought leadership initiative is being able to capitalize on the positives and mitigate the negatives. This requires that you scrupulously evaluate how your firm's thought leadership initiative is progressing and how it can be improved (see *Appendix A: Money Rules*). The following question will likely prove helpful (see Exhibit 7.4):

- *Where are the successes and failures?* Your firm should perpetually be examining each phase and each set of actions to see what is working well and what isn't. Doing so often abates the likelihood of severe complications later on.

- *What can you learn from the failures?* As you'll very likely find glitches in your firm's thought leadership initiative, your firm needs to be able to act expeditiously to mitigate adverse results. At the same time, by carefully evaluating these speed bumps, your firm can determine how to do much better the next time around.

- *How can your successes yield greater returns?* Your firm should critically dissect the actions that worked very well to generate even better results. There will be ways to raise the positives to a higher level—an obvious objective.

EXHIBIT 7.4: REFINING THE THOUGHT LEADERSHIP INITIATIVE

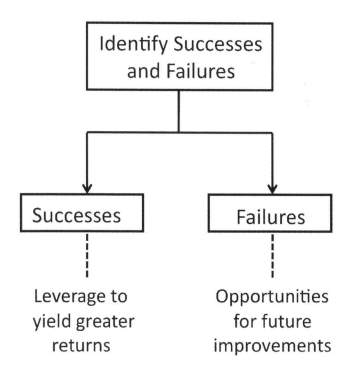

What's essential to refining any professional services firm's thought leadership initiative is keeping a clear and persistent eye on the financial returns of the endeavor. The motivation, as we see it, for being a thought leader is business development, and that means more revenues. Hence, all efforts at refining must be tightly interrelated with achieving the financial end goal (see *Chapter 9: Monetizing*).

FOOD FOR THOUGHT

We've seen more than a handful of professional services firms jump headfirst into becoming a thought leader without anything resembling a strategy. Some of the managing partners we've dealt with fail to credit the sophistication required of a top-flight thought leadership initiative, which is why support from the right managing partners championing the efforts is often critical.

In our experience, while the enthusiasm of managing partners is usually great, it's sometimes all rah-rah without a substantial strategy backed by requisite resources. As a result, we've often ended up going round in circles. Not thinking through in advance as many things as possible tends to result in jumping off the highest diving board into an empty pool.

It's the anomalous thought leadership initiative that achieves all or even most of its goals without a goodly amount of deft modifications and tweaking along the way. Nevertheless, thinking through the issues brought up herein goes an awfully long way toward attaining the best results possible.

INTERLUDE: NAVIGATING THE FUTURE OF MEDICINE

DANIEL CARLIN M.D., CEO AND FOUNDER, WORLDCLINIC

At 6'3" with salt and pepper hair, Dan's usually easy to spot in a crowd. He's very affable and easygoing. He's gregarious and friendly, qualities that belie his encyclopedic knowledge of geography, medicine and technology. Dan's something of a 21st century Marcus Welby, providing Dr. Welby was able to deliver the most sophisticated medical solutions to his patients, anytime and anywhere in the world.

Dan founded WorldClinic in 1998, drawing on years of experience as a medical officer in the US Navy and later as an expatriate volunteer. What started off as a medical service for affluent families living a global lifestyle has evolved into one of the most sophisticated medical practices on Earth.

WorldClinic is internationally recognized as one of the finest healthcare concierge companies today. The firm has combined a physician care team with a "total care" platform that provides a broad array of healthcare services including 24/7 tele-medical diagnosis and treatment, complex disease management, medical contingency planning and provisioning, aeromedical evacuations and maintaining accurate long-term electronic medical records.

WorldClinic is spearheading the use of advanced tele-medicine assessment and treatment methodologies. For example, they are setting the standard in providing connected clients with guided emergency care 24/7 no matter where they are on the planet. This asset is of critical importance for dealing with an emergency's "Golden Hour"—that short period of time when medical treatment or lack thereof can literally mean the difference between life and death.

The firm is also leading the way in the use of cutting-edge diagnostics such as biomarkers as part of its state-of-the-art longevity program. These predictive assessments offer the opportunity to take preventive actions now in order to avoid possible severe medical problems later in life.

Dan's focus has always been squarely on delivering the finest in top-notch medical care to WorldClinic's clients. However, being an exceptional physician and even putting together a well-oiled firm of outstanding medical, technological and support talent, does not necessarily result in the business being a big hit. It's not enough to be the foremost concierge healthcare firm if your "ideal prospects" don't know that you are.

What transformed Dan's business was that he started freely communicating the firm's leveraging concepts, and even the methodologies, that are transforming the field of medicine. Through articles, reports, interviews and speaking engagements, Dan is sharing the future of medicine and the actions that can result in people living substantially longer and healthier lives. In addition, the firm commits significant resources to garnering a deep understanding of its ultra-successful clients such as family offices, CEOs, board members and the super-rich. These research efforts extend to lifestyle issues and concerns beyond the realm of medicine. What has proven valuable is that WorldClinic has chosen to share these findings and insights for the benefit of their clients as well as the clients of other professionals. It's the sharing by WorldClinic of its intellectual capital that has been so instrumental in making the leading concierge healthcare provider a significantly more famous and profitable business.

The big difference, producing an immense financial payoff, is that Dan stood up and shared WorldClinic's intellectual capital. In so doing, the firm rapidly became an industry thought leader to the ultra-successful and the professionals who work with these highly accomplished individuals. Based on their commanding lead as experts in concierge healthcare coupled with their willingness to share, WorldClinic will soon join the ranks of celebrity industry thought leaders.

CHAPTER 8:
PRODUCTIZING

From strategizing we move to productizing. The result of this phase of the thought leadership process is for your professional services firm to create and distribute high-quality thought leadership products to select audiences. While we've been using the term thought leadership products throughout, it actually refers to the final result of the productizing phase.

Productizing starts with the unearthing of intellectual capital. This raw material is then processed and refined into thought leadership content. Lastly, the thought leadership content is made tangible as thought leadership products. The distribution strategies are built into the thought leadership products.

Thought leadership products can be an unlimited renewable resource, but this isn't automatically the case. While an abundance of possibilities can be the basis for intellectual capital that you can convert into thought leadership content and thence into thought leadership products, it's important to ascertain the ones that can most profitably fuel your firm's thought leadership initiative—the ones that result in the creation of exceptional new business opportunities.

The direction professional services firms should take are predicated on the target audiences. You should consider the following two questions as your firm develops its thought leadership initiative:

Question 1: Does your firm want to concentrate on clients and prospects, referral sources or both?

Question 2: How will the firm's designated domain expertise tie into the thought leadership products?

Staying attuned to the audience a thought leadership initiative is intended to serve, coupled with how it relates to the firm's expertise, best positions your firm to potentially capitalize on its efforts. With all the various goals in mind—especially the financial end goal—it's essential to make sure the brilliance your firm can deliver finds a responsive audience and is thereby exceptionally profitable. So when the expertise and capabilities are overlaid on the target audiences, it's exactly on point.

In this chapter we're going to crudely—by necessity—dissect the productizing phase, as we're doing to the thought leadership process itself. While it's a complicated and intricate phase, simplified productizing consists of three interconnected components (see Exhibit 8.1):

- Identification.
- Transformation.
- Communication.

EXHIBIT 8.1: THE COMPONENTS OF PRODUCTIZING

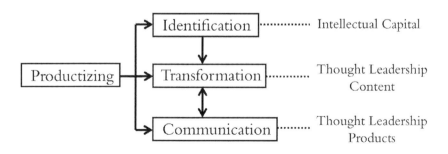

Let's delve a little into each of them.

IDENTIFICATION

At this point, your professional services firm needs to develop the underpinning for the thought leadership initiative—the intellectual capital. This can be the make-or-break element of any thought leadership initiative. No matter how well the intellectual capital is packaged, unless real value underpins the firm's thought leadership products, they will not resonate very well with the target audiences.

A very effective way to start unearthing the intellectual capital is to decide on the broad-based audience—clients compared to referral sources—and to decide on the focus on the thought leadership initiative. Very simply, while not exclusive, there are two principle alternatives when it comes to focus (see Exhibit 8.2):

- *Solution-focused.* The intellectual capital is of the how-to variety. It's all about clients or referral sources getting specific results. As part of the how to your firm is seeking to deliver, the four Ws are often critically important—what to, when to, why to and where to. With this approach, the professional services firms can most effectively and meaningfully connect its expertise to the needs and wants of the audiences.
- *Perspective-focused.* The intellectual capital in addressing current or projected states. Examples of this include industry insights, trends and forecasts. What is essential to make this approach viable is the analysis that augments the descriptions. It's this analysis that makes the professional services firm a thought leader. As this approach is often heavily opinion-based, it might or might not be directly tied to the expertise of a professional services firm.

EXHIBIT 8.2: THE FOCUS OF THE INTELLECTUAL CAPITAL

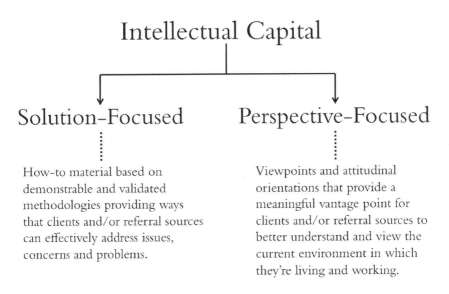

Intellectual Capital

Solution-Focused

How-to material based on demonstrable and validated methodologies providing ways that clients and/or referral sources can effectively address issues, concerns and problems.

Perspective-Focused

Viewpoints and attitudinal orientations that provide a meaningful vantage point for clients and/or referral sources to better understand and view the current environment in which they're living and working.

For many professional services firms, a crucial factor in deciding whether to go with solution-focused versus perspective-focused intellectual capital is the extent to which the firm wants to connect its specializations with the thought leadership initiative. Additionally, windows of opportunity such as changing regulations and changing economic conditions make being perspective-focused very worthwhile.

Having decided which direction to take, there are quite a number of places your firm can look for the possibilities that you can convert into intellectual capital (see Exhibit 8.3). One of the first places we recommend considering is within the professional services firm itself. Some examples of this include:

- The professionals within the firm.
- The staff.
- Other professionals, especially referral sources.
- The experiences and preferences of clients.

Your firm can also tap into panoply of open sources to identify ideas and hypotheses. Some of these are:

- The media.
- The relevant professional literature.
- Core ideas from other disciplines.
- Industry analysts and consultants.
- Leading authorities from completely different industries.

EXHIBIT 8.3: SOURCES FOR POSSIBILITIES

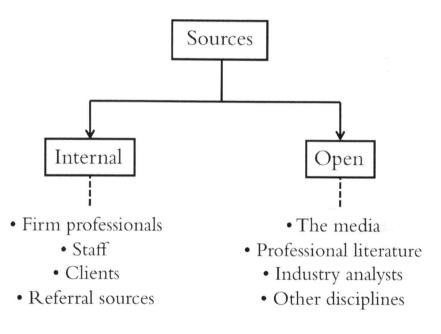

Now you need to convert these possibilities into intellectual capital. What's required is the application of a high level of analytic ability to discerning critical and audience-viable patterns that can be the prima materia for thought leadership products. There are quite a number of ways to facilitate the conversion of raw perspectives into intellectual capital. Two approaches often used—sometimes in concert—are concept-generation techniques and market research.

Concept-generation techniques. Intellectual capital is often the identification of new concepts or, more often, the recombination of commonly understood, recognized and already validated concepts. The adroit and clever reformulation is what makes the old new and appealing to the target audiences. Both groups and individuals can use these techniques.

Brainstorming, for example, is one of the most widely and effectively employed concept-generation techniques. This is where the participants adhere to a clearly delineated set of conventions and procedures to come up with the variables, considerations and forces that can convert possibilities into intellectual capital. The group can be prompted in many ways to come up with possibilities, including:

- *Transposition of rated source material.* You can collect ideas and positions from other various sources—internal and open—which you evaluate and, when appropriate, map and reformulate.
- *Exploit analogies.* Consideration of possible similarities to other situations in time or in other industries can often prove quite useful in moving brainstorming sessions along.
- *Leverage social science.* Various social science perspectives can provide expected causalities, projections and predictions. These perspectives can be assessed in the brainstorming sessions for applicability and viability.

There are many ways to enhance traditional brainstorming sessions. For instance, using a wiki can augment these sessions. A wiki easily permits the participants to collect and merge the results of the session, as well as providing an ongoing mechanism to continue the brainstorming sessions even when the participants are geographically dispersed.

Another way to enhance brainstorming session is to use on-point impact matrices. They regularly prove useful as a supporting technique or follow-up to brainstorming. The objective is to have managing partners and other participants in the brainstorming sessions determine how different variables will affect each other within pre-set parameters. Very often we find that this approach leads to reconfiguring material.

Market research. Quantitative and qualitative research is often used to identify, develop and refine intellectual capital. It can be used to distinguish your professional services firm from others by enabling your firm to go beyond anecdotes and personal interpretations of situations and circumstances. Market research serves a number of functions when it comes to intellectual capital, including:

- *Validation.* When certain premises and conclusions raise questions and have doubters, market research can corroborate those conclusions. It's a matter of providing proof for ideas and positions that many, but not all, will accept.
- *Quantification.* Many find it comforting when objectivity, in the form of numbers, is attached to perspectives. Another aspect of this is when levels and intensities are delineated.
- *Distillation.* This practice marginally refines possibilities. It's where a certain amount of digging into a data set results in synthesizing the information creating cohesion.
- *Interpretation.* Here new intellectual capital is found within the data set. This can be a byproduct of the market research or the intent of the researchers.

While not always a possibility or applicable, market research can serve a myriad of purposes in unearthing and enhancing meaningful and functional intellectual capital. As empiricists, we're admittedly biased in favor of well-done market research as the underpinning of high-quality intellectual capital that can be converted into thought leadership content and then into thought leadership products.

Over decades, we've been extensively involved in conducting research to identify, validate and refine intellectual capital. We've employed both quantitative and qualitative methodologies (see Exhibit 8.4).

EXHIBIT 8.4: TYPES OF MARKET RESEARCH

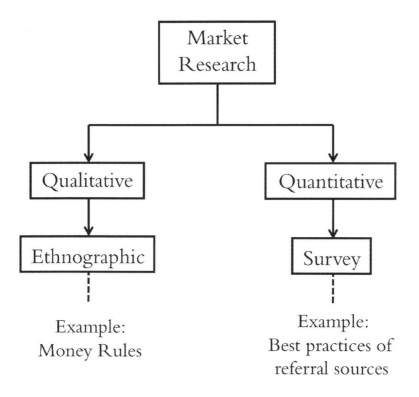

Surveys of the business processes of referral sources, for example, can result in the foundation for "best practices" thought leadership products. This can be a cornerstone of that aspect of your firm's dual-impact brand addressing referral sources. It can also be used as currency to help motivate referral sources to provide your firm with astounding introductions. Along the same lines, surveys of the ways prospects and clients are dealing with select problematic situations is regularly very effective in setting the stage to discuss particular expertise your firm can provide.

An example of qualitative research is how the self-made super-rich amassed their fortunes (see *Appendix A: Money Rules*). These rules of conduct are predicated on ethnological research with the self-made super-rich, where we were able to distill their mindset and behavior into a pattern that other people can replicate. There are a variety of qualitative research methodologies. Focus groups, for example, are commonly employed in this regard.

Like seeking to become a thought leader, using market research to generate intellectual capital is not a new approach. On the contrary, it's the basis of a great deal of intellectual capital that's later massaged into thought leadership content and products. Clearly, market research is a tried-and-true, extensively employed approach to creating, validating and refining ideas and concepts, processes and systems. When done well, a research-based thought leadership initiative can be an exceptionally powerful way to become a commanding industry presence.

Because high-caliber market research can pave the way to becoming a thought leader and even a celebrity thought leader, a lot of professional services firms are using this approach. This is resulting in an absolute glut of market research efforts. With so many crowding the dance floor, few have the room to shine. In this heated contest, the winner will be the professional services firm that not only uses the research to find or validate intellectual capital, but is able to transform that intellectual capital into thought leadership content, which subsequently becomes high-quality thought leadership products.

TRANSFORMATION

The next step, therefore, is transforming the intellectual capital into thought leadership content. Your firm needs to convert the intellectual capital into multilayered, often interconnected, actionable strategies and tactics that meet the needs and wants of your target audiences—prospects and clients and/or referral sources. When it comes to this step, the essence of an effective transition from intellectual capital to thought leadership content is applicability. In converting the intellectual capital into thought leadership content, your firm is:

- Forming a sense, coalesced into manageable patterns, of the way critical aspects of the business world operate.
- Creating a set of well-formulated archetypes, each inherently embedded with meaning.
- Providing an easy-to-appreciate amalgam of solutions or collection of topical facts and/or trends.

A good way to think about thought leadership content is as touchstone themes, clearly articulated storylines that meld into a cohesive and persuasive whole. As such, thought leadership content can be cut up and repurposed into many thought leadership products. With well-conceptualized thought leadership content, your firm is converting the storylines supported by all the associated elements and floating components into readily accessible formats—thought leadership products—for each targeted audience (see Exhibit 8.5).

EXHIBIT 8.5: TRANSFORMATION

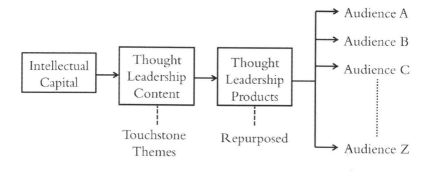

With the touchstone themes identified and refined, your firm must package the thought leadership content into thought leadership products. Now it's really all about packaging. It's often useful to consider the following:

- How are the target audience members most likely to consume the thought leadership content?
- How extensively and far can the thought leadership content be repurposed and stretched?
- How much flexibility and plasticity can be built into the thought leadership product portfolio without diminishing the value of the thought leadership content?

By adding physicality to the thought leadership content, you're developing thought leadership products. Here, the intangible is made tangible; the amorphous is made solid. Now we're dealing with how something is said as opposed to what is being said. It's about aesthetics. It's about "feel." It's about engaging by design. It's about "chunking" the storylines, thereby making them easy to digest and assimilate. Very often, the process of packaging the thought leadership content is an interactive one that's tied into the way your firm intends to distribute the information (see below).

Inherent in the packaging is a call to action. As we've defined the term and process, thought leadership doesn't exist without monetization (see *Chapter 3: What Is a Thought Leader?*, *Chapter 4: The Case for Thought Leadership* and *Coda: The Future of Profitable Brilliance*). This isn't possible unless in cleverly calibrating the touchstone themes that are the basis for the thought leadership products, your professional services firm is building in a need for clients, prospects and referral sources to connect back with your firm.

COMMUNICATION

Preferably, the way for professional services firms to build a very loyal following based on thought leadership is by having the desired clients and referral sources find them. This is in many respects a highly prosperous, marvelously cost-effective self-selection process. It's the difference between sales and marketing where garnering very loyal followers is unquestionably a well-articulated marketing process.

Members of your target audiences will gravitate to your firm's thought leadership products. They will evaluate the thought leadership content and determine if it's viable and beneficial for them. Part of that decision-making process is the cost and the audience's ability to receive the same or comparable thought leadership content from other sources. What's important is to recognize that your professional services firm needs to strongly and expeditiously capitalize on the audience's self-selection progression.

This self-selection progression is commonly referred to as the filtering process (see Exhibit 8.6). It's a three-stage process that starts with the total potential audience and is eventually narrowed down to the very loyal followers. What helps winnow out the total audience to a smaller number of followers and then to an even smaller group of very loyal followers is a willingness and ability to pay for the thought leadership content, coupled with the professional services firm's capacity to deliver enhanced thought leadership products to clients and referral sources that are progressing through the three stages.

As the audience goes through each stage, people drop out until your firm is left with a small cadre of very loyal followers. For those members of the audience that first respond to the thought leadership products, they enter Stage I: Experimentation. Here the audience is becoming familiar with your firm's thought leadership content through one or a number of its thought leadership products. The audience members are starting to evaluate its relevance and applicability in their own environments and situations. You're finding audience members who are interested in what your firm is offering. Those audience members who value the thought leadership products favorably continue on. Meanwhile, a percentage of the target audience drops off.

In Stage II: Focused Adoption, the remaining audience members are seriously integrating key ideas, themes and models into their worlds. They have vetted the thought leadership products and deemed them worthwhile. The professional services firm can now consider these audience members its followers. It's common for many audience members to stay at this stage. On a situational basis, they will work with the professional services firm or refer clients to the firm. Because they are generating significant revenues for the professional services firm, that firm has become a thought leader.

When the professional services firm is able to deliver new and/ or enhanced versions or applications of the thought leadership content, the audience is generally inclined to progress faster through the process. If this is the case, what tends to happen is that more audience members respond positively to the professional services firm and they're more inclined to pay for the continuum of thought leadership products.

As the professional services firm becomes the near-exclusive go-to provider for its expertise, the audience members have entered Stage III: Internalization. The value added in the form of thought leadership products provided by the professional services firm for these audience members is so substantial that the firm heads the list of providers and, barring doing something horrendous, pretty consistently wins the business. At this point, the audience members can be considered very loyal followers, and the professional services firm has become a celebrity thought leader.

EXHIBIT 8.6: THE FILTERING PROCESS

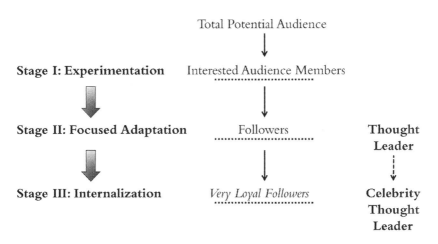

As noted, the transformation stage and the communication stage are intimately entwined. Nevertheless, whereas we can separate the two stages, at this juncture we'll address a few of the ways thought leadership content is delivered. Specifically, we'll consider:

- Packaged content.
- Live events.
- Social media.

Packaged content. Making thought leadership content tangible has historically been achieved, and today is still accomplished, by concerting the touchstone themes into the likes of:

- Bylined articles.
- Firm-produced reports.
- Books.

Very often the move is up the spectrum because of time to market and the requisite substance (see Exhibit 8.7). The goal is to continually leverage up. So, while the first collection of thought leadership products follows this progression, the professional services firm then needs to capitalize on the traction it's getting by repurposing the released thought leadership products, often including additional material to continue the progression.

EXHIBIT 8.7: WRITTEN PACKAGED CONTENT

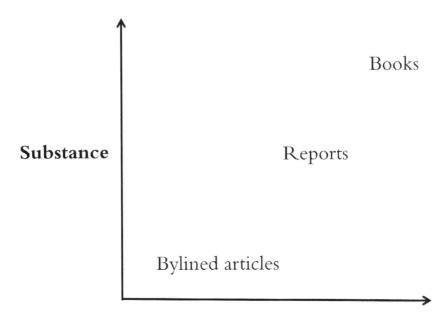

Another effective way to package the thought leadership content is as advertorials. One of the critical keys to making an advertorial highly effective is to ensure that it powerfully highlights one dazzling piece of thought leadership content and that it offers a built-in rationale for the interested reader to connect with the professional services firm. It's also quite useful to run an array of advertorial variations revolving around one or two touchstone themes.

Podcasts, for select audiences, are proving to be an increasingly effective way to package thought leadership content. The advantages of the Internet with audio and video components are making podcasts particularly appealing to both clients and referral sources.

The most underused form of packaged content today is e-learning programs. These are multifaceted educational courses delivered through the Internet. While all thought leadership content can be converted into e-learning programs, because of the cost involved, it's generally advisable to run the numbers and project the payoff from the effort.

You have access to an entire menu of instructional options when constructing e-learning programs. They can have many of the same involvement elements as live events (see below). They can be unidirectional or highly interactive. They can be designed for individuals or for groups. With the considerable flexibility inherent in the construction of e-learning programs, the professional services firm must be very focused on its financial end goal, its strategic end goals and especially its intermediary goals (see *Chapter 7: Strategizing*).

If an e-learning program can be a certificate program awarded by an accredited school of higher education, so much the better. This is especially useful as it provides a standard, as well as setting the stage for future learning and consequentially a stronger ongoing relationship with the professional services firm.

The nature of packaged content is going to radically change over the next few years. E-books, for example, are likely to replace printed books as powerful thought leadership products. E-books will be very useful for building bridges to clients and referral sources. What we'll probably see is that Internet-predicated interactive capabilities will significantly augment the traditional packaged content. All in all, the use of evolving communication technologies, including the likes of apps and various mobile tools, will revolutionize the nature of packaged content.

Live Events. From the perspective of business development, it's often critical to "press the flesh." Optimally, the goal is one-to-one (also team-to-team) meetings (see *Chapter 9: Monetizing*). However, a solid intermediary step and a very potent way to communicate your firm's thought leadership content is by participating in events.

The various types of events have different goals and differential potentials in engendering loyalty (see Exhibit 8.8). The ability to transition prospects from the less influential events to the more influential events is often a strategic objective, and doing so is highly conducive to becoming a thought leader or enhancing the firm's positioning as such.

EXHIBIT 8.8: EVENT POSSIBILITIES BROADLY DEFINED

Type of Event	Common Durations	Ease of Execution	Ability to Cultivate Loyalty
Meal-based meetings	A few hours	Easy	Low
Workshops	A few hours to multiple days	Somewhat Problematic	Medium
Conferences	One or more days	Problematic	Medium
Symposiums	One or more days	Somewhat Difficult	Medium
Training Sessions	One or more days	Difficult	High
Coaching Programs	Scattered in multiple sessions	Very Difficult	Very High

Not only is the quality of the thought leadership content a critical component of any live event, but also the ability to present the material in an engaging and motivating manner is usually crucial. Consider all the business presentations you've sat through.

- How many of these business presentations were engaging?
- How many times were you regretful that the presenter was finished?
- How many times did you walk away feeling that your time was very well spent?
- How many of these business presentations provided really useful information?
- How many times were you seriously impressed with the presenter's knowledge and delivery?

In our experience, we've found that most professionals are not the most polished orators. Now, we're not claiming that the presenters need to be dazzlingly captivating speakers. A charismatic delivery would be nice, but it's not required. However, the presenters do need to be comfortable and proficient in front of an audience. It's also very advantageous if presenters are able to "dance"—can gauge and work off the audience—even a little. For many professionals who are not strong public speakers, the answer lies in a combination of instruction and practice.

Social media. Where the communications are web-based and possibly mobile, and the intent is to create a community of like-minded individuals, we have the fast-changing and potentially confusing world of social media. The creation of a community helps in fostering user-generated content that other members of the community share and potentially adjust or add to. There are many different forms of social media, including:

- Forums.
- Blogs of various designs.
- Collaborative projects.

- Wikis.
- Community networking sites.

In the context of thought leadership, the complication with much of social media is one of identifying and maintaining the designated expert. The objective of any thought leadership initiative is to crown key Savants within the professional services firm as the undisputed designated experts. This positioning can quite easily be lost when multiple authorities weigh in on trends, issues and perspectives. It's a matter of how much of the position of specialist the professional services firm is willing to share.

One way to conceptualize and think about this conundrum is to consider the matter from two interacting vantage points—the nature of the thought leadership content and the types of audiences (see Exhibit 8.9). Generally speaking, the more the thought leadership content connects to the firm's expertise, the less likely it is that today's social media will be the most viable medium.

The least applicable use of social media is when the audiences are clients and the thought leadership content is solution-focused. Conversely, the most applicable use of social media is when the audiences are clients and the thought leadership content is perspective-focused. When it comes to referral sources, whether the thought leadership content is solution-focused or perspective-focused, the applicability of social media ranges.

EXHIBIT 8.9: CONNECTIONS TO THE FIRM'S EXPERTISE

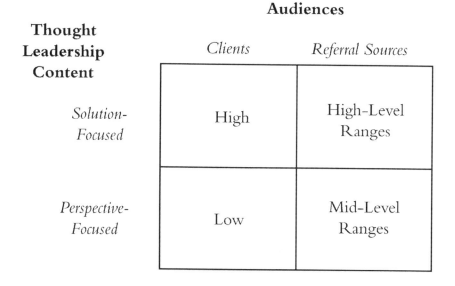

While professional services firms seeking to become thought leaders will certainly increasingly embrace the evolving social media platforms, currently there often isn't a clear way to connect all the dots effectively, thereby ensuring that the many benefits of being a thought leader are tied to the firm, as opposed to marginalization of the firm and/or hijacking of the advantages gained from the thought leadership content. A lot of experimentation and practice is still needed to make the platforms and tools of social media powerful components of a thought leadership initiative.

The underlying issue that requires resolution is, per thought leadership initiative, where to find the efficacious sweet spot on the spectrum of unidirectionality to total audience participation. It's inevitable, however, that professional services firms will harvest social media and its technologies in their efforts to become thought leaders.

FOOD FOR THOUGHT

The productizing phase is going to become much more sophisticated going forward. There are a few key drivers for this:

- A growing need to dig deeper and unearth powerful intellectual capital that can be refined using more-complex analytic tools and techniques into ever higher-quality thought leadership content and then into more influential thought leadership products.
- Technological changes resulting in new and more powerful pedagogical approaches that can be ever more individualized.
- Competitive pressures, a function of the ultra competitive environment professional services firms find themselves in today, are made more arduous by a generally more discerning clientele.

The nature of the thought leadership products, while holding to their center, will evolve dramatically in form and structure. We touched on the advantages of e-books over printed books. The development of apps is becoming normative, with quite a few professional services firms joining—or attempting to join—the crowd. The use of social media is a relatively untapped communication strategy. But for social media to reach its potential in this context, it will likely require the development of different modalities of thought leadership products.

While it's not necessary to be an innovator when it comes to creating thought leadership products, in many circumstances it will be essential to be a fast follower. This is a risk-mitigation approach that can enable a professional services firm to more cost-effectively become a thought leader and potentially a celebrity thought leader. On the other hand, if your firm can innovate effectively, it will likely tremendously speed up its ascension to the status of thought leader and celebrity thought leader.

INTERLUDE: THE BUSINESS COACH

BRETT VAN BORTELL, DIRECTOR OF CONSULTING SERVICES, INVESCO

Wholesaling financial products such as mutual funds and exchange traded funds is a highly competitive business. Financial advisors have thousands of options across a wide variety of investment companies to choose from. Many of the funds have solid performance and good track records, making it all the harder for the investment companies to meaningfully differentiate their offerings from the competition. That's where Brett and his colleagues at Invesco Consulting come in.

In the world of investment management companies and value-added wholesaling, Invesco Consulting is at the standard competitors all compare themselves to. Under the direction of Scott West and with the assistance of Gary DeMoss, the consulting group has established itself as the recognized leader in developing thought leadership materials and using these materials to enable financial advisors reach new levels of success by sharpening their client focus. In so doing, Invesco Consulting dominates the field of value-added wholesaling.

Talking to most anyone in the business of wholesaling investment products to financial advisors and it's clear that Invesco Consulting has become the foremost authority and resource in their specialty. Value-added wholesaling is where the investment company—aside from trying to provide the very best investment products—actively looks for ways to enable financial advisors to be more successful.

What's the rationale for this wholesaling approach? It's very straightforward. When a financial advisor needs to select an investment product for a client, the advisor will select the investment product from the investment company providing the "extra" value. This is the case as long as the investment product in question is of very high quality. When different investment products are fairly evenly matched with respect to performance, financial advisors will indeed select those products for their clients from the investment company providing the most viable and usable value-added expertise.

Value-added wholesaling makes a difference at the margins. And it's at the margins where tremendous differences occur between the financial performance of most investment companies. Generally, no matter how good the practice management material an investment company provides, if its products are substandard, financial advisors are not going to use them with their clients. However, since many investment products are indeed on the same plane, value-added wholesaling has become an area that can help an investment management company stand out with advisors in a resoundingly positive way.

Brett is instrumental in developing and communicating some of the most effective programs constructed in the industry. He has been key to some of Invesco's most successful programs. For example, Rainmaker provides a well-structured and carefully delineated roadmap for garnering new affluent clients from other professionals. Another massive success has been Wealth Mapping. Here the financial advisors learn to identify all the various ways they can deliver exceptional value to high-net-worth clients.

Aside from being adept at standing up and conveying the strategies and tactics that can enable financial advisors to reach dramatically new plateaus of success, Brett regularly gets into the trenches and works with select financial advisory teams to transform critical aspects of their businesses, thereby fast-tacking them to ever higher levels of accomplishment. Without question, in world of financial advisors, Brett is considered one of the leading business coaches around.

What makes Brett and Invesco Consulting so effective is their ability to truly listen to financial advisors and drill down to identify the big issues they face. They're able to marshal the best talents available from inside and outside the company to develop thought leadership materials that strongly resonate with their target audience—the financial advisor. Very importantly, as spearheaded by Brett, they can work with financial advisors in all types of venues from large audiences to one-on-one sessions to make the thought leadership material powerful and impactful.

CHAPTER 9:
MONETIZING

Why become a thought leader, let alone a celebrity thought leader? It's time-consuming and generally an awful lot of hard work. It can often be costly, and (take our word for it) it's regularly aggravating in so very many ways. From a business perspective, the reason so many managing partners at professional services firms seek to become a thought leader—and preferably a celebrity thought leader—is the payoff.

Being a thought leader is evidenced by considerable commercial success.

When a professional services firm transitions from a Hidden Talent to a Talented Expert, the financial returns can be mind-boggling (to put it mildly). At the very least, when done well, thought leadership initiatives pay for themselves a multitude of times over their all-in costs. However, for the financial payday to come along, your firm has to be very tightly focused on profiting from the endeavor.

It's all about crossing the finish line. Better yet, it's about crossing the finish line first. When it comes to thought leadership, we're referring to very successful business development that's a result of the skilled distribution and follow-up of high-quality thought leadership products.

There's also the option of making money by being paid directly for your firm's thought leadership products. However, as we'll come to understand, this option is not the preferred or optimal one for the vast majority of professional services firms.

FOLLOWING UP

This phase of the thought leadership process deals with following up after the provisioning of thought leadership products. This is the part of the thought leadership process that deals extensively with generating additional revenues.

Without well-orchestrated follow-up, there's a diminished possibility of making money. That's not to say the thought leadership initiative wouldn't stalwartly buff a professional services firm's brand, which in turn helps cultivate new clients as well as more business from existing clients. It's also not to say that the thought leadership initiative wouldn't bring in new business over the transom. There's plenty of proof that both these scenarios will indeed occur. However, while getting new engagements these ways is a good thing, if your firm really wants to sincerely and dramatically benefit from being a thought leader, the professionals therein must subsequently reach out actively to clients, prospects and referral sources.

For the most part, the professionals at your firm cannot convert a prospect into a client without having some sort of direct contact. Even in situations where there are requests for proposals, after the proposals have been winnowed down to a small number, the client usually wants an in-person presentation or meeting of some sort.

Now, there are times when prospects will buy a professional services firm sight unseen—so to speak. We have seen this happen periodically—for example, when referral sources have such a powerful relationship with the client that their recommendations are taken without much questioning. However, it's much more common for prospects to want to meet and personally judge for themselves the professionals they will potentially hire.

Critical to follow-up is getting the in-person meeting with the prospect. Being a thought leader is very much about making it both easier and much more common to get those meetings on a very preferential basis. For each thought leadership product, there's a built-in stratagem to:

- Create a situation where prospects, clients and referral sources want more.
- Meet in person to make it clear that your professional services firm is able to provide more in a variety of ways.

It's at this point—when the professional meets with the prospect—that the prospect must be convinced to do business. Similarly, when the professional meets with referral sources, they must be convinced to send their clients over. When used properly, thought leadership products such as articles, reports and books prove very helpful as support tools in converting a prospect into a client. Nevertheless, at some point, the professionals involved have to close.

THE OFTEN PERVASIVE FAILURE TO FOLLOW UP AND CLOSE

Before it's possible to close, professionals from your firm have to meet the prospects and potential referral sources—the defining benefit of being a thought leader. However, when handed warm leads and opportunities to move business relationships forward, the professionals must take action. Regrettably, it's not uncommon for professionals to be less than assertive when it comes to follow-up. Just consider:

- Has your firm ever held an event where few if any of the firm's professionals attended?
- Has your firm ever held an event where the firm's professionals spent the time talking among themselves?
- Has your firm ever held an event without a prearranged strategy of what to do after the event?

Many professionals are not very adept at closing, whether they look at selling as anathema, or they are willing but lack the knowledge and skill. Think of all the professionals at your firm—who can do a top-notch job of converting a prospect to a client and who is less proficient? Along the same lines, what's also all too common is a discomfort in reaching out to prospects and referral sources even when they're clearly interested.

We've been involved in thought leadership initiatives for professional services firms that have crashed and burned because the professionals involved failed to follow up. Thought leadership products will rarely prompt new engagements unless the professionals follow up.

At a major conference where the law firm spent a great deal of money to put on an event, for instance, all the attorneys from the firm talked to each other throughout the proceedings. After the event, they all went out to dinner together and congratulated themselves on filling the entire room with qualified prospects. While there are quite a few missteps here, the biggest issue is that they didn't take advantage of the opportunity to garner new business, which was the entire purpose of the event.

Not only should there be well-structured and organized post-event follow-up, to maximize those opportunities, the lawyers at the event should be prescreening and evaluating attendees. There are quite a few ways to achieve this, including:

- Creating a database profiling attendees in advance.
- Arming the professionals working the event with profiling questions.
- Arranging for select additional material to be provided to attendees, but only if they request them.

Keep in mind that the filtering process (see *Chapter 8: Productizing*) will screen and motivate highly qualified prospects and referral sources. This can all be accomplished by providing a gradually amassed collection of more intensive and content-laden thought leadership products. Still, to move from potential to actual, from prospects to clients, requires the professionals to follow up and close.

Any thought leadership initiative is a failure if it doesn't result in seriously above-average return on investment. All the most virtuoso and inspired strategizing and productizing will mean nothing without monetizing. So if the professionals at your firm lack the ability or drive to follow up and close, there are two options:

- Teach them how to follow up and close.
- Find other people who can follow up and close.

All marketing activities should be evaluated with respect to their cost and effectiveness. Thought leadership initiatives are no exception.

CALCULATING SUCCESS (AND FAILURE)

Every marketing endeavor should be critically evaluated, and that includes thought leadership initiatives. There is an abundance of ways to calculate success and failure, with the following ones high on the list:

- Comparisons to goals.
- Comparisons to other business development activities.

Let's consider each of these types of comparisons (see Exhibit 9.1).

EXHIBIT 9.1: SUCCESSES AND FAILURES

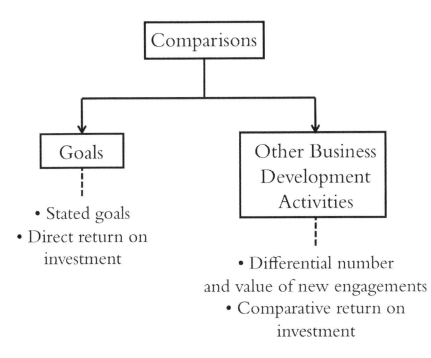

Comparisons to goals. In the first and ongoing phase of the thought leadership process—strategizing—the managing partners of the firm identified a financial end goal as well as strategic and intermediary goals (see *Chapter 7: Strategizing*). Here, the firm benefits by taking those various goals into account and continues to compare its results to those goals.

As part of this comparison, it's often useful to incorporate a direct return on investment calculation. Achieving the desired financial end goal is not all that impressive if the price is too high. Real financial success requires a solid pecuniary return for the time, effort and resources committed to the thought leadership initiative.

This perpetual feedback is central to refining and improving the current thought leadership initiative as well as providing valuable lessons for future thought leadership initiatives. As we noted in the very beginning of this treatise, much of our education and proficiencies with respect to helping professional services firms become thought leaders is a function of a great deal of experience. In the early years, more than a few times our experiences turned out to be less than positive. Having carefully autopsied the failures and learned from them, we became quite adept at implementing each phase of the thought leadership process (see *Appendix A: Money Rules*).

Comparisons to other business development activities. It often proves very instructive to see how a thought leadership initiative matches up to other business development activities. This will enable your firm to better gauge the viability of its thought leadership initiatives, including making the most of your firm's marketing dollars.

The complication is that there can be, and often is, overlap between the components of a thought leadership campaign and various other business development activities. Nevertheless, to the extent that lines of demarcation can be drawn, we regularly find that thought leadership initiatives, while taking some time to mature and generate results, are the superior marketing approach for many professional services firms.

EXHIBIT 9.2: DIRECT COMPENSATION

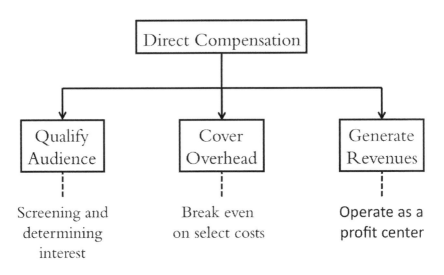

GETTING DIRECTLY COMPENSATED

The overwhelming predominant payment to professional services firms for sensational thought leadership products is the firm's extensive access to well-qualified, high-caliber prospects. In many situations involving referral sources, for example, your firm's thought leadership products act as a form of currency. As such, providing thought leadership products in accord with a dual-impact brand could be very motivating to referral sources.

Another way for a professional services firm to be compensated for it's thought leadership products is directly—that is, the audience buys the products. This may involve purchasing books and reports or attending workshops. The costs attached to thought leadership products tend to fall into three nonexclusive categories (see Exhibit 9.2):

- *Intended to qualify the audience.* Charging for thought leadership products could prove instrumental in screening the audience. Those individuals and firms that are particularly interested and will likely be most responsive will be most inclined to pay.

- *Intended to cover overhead.* Charging attendees a fee can offset the cost of workshops. Those who attend and pay to do so are more likely to be motivated to do business with your firm. The fee, however, is relatively minor, with the intent of enabling the workshop or other thought leadership product to break even.

- *Intended to generate revenues.* Providing thought leadership products with the intent of making a profit—and possibly a substantial one—is a business model tangential to sourcing clients. However, explicitly intending to generate revenues will not necessarily detract from the professional services firm's ability to garner new business for its expertise.

The decisions surrounding whether and how to be compensated are best resolved by assessing the business development opportunities and matching them with the complications and cost structure of the thought leadership initiative or campaign, taking into account your firm's strategic objectives. Basically, this is all wrapped into running the numbers (see *Chapter 6: The Thought Leadership Process*).

Even in situations where the audience pays for the thought leadership products, the costs tend to be minimal. By and large, the primary objective of professional services firms in becoming thought leaders is to source exceptional clients.

REFINEMENT AND PROOF

As we say in *Chapter 6: The Thought Leadership Process*, there's a feedback loop between monetizing and strategizing. Meaningfully improving your firm's ability to become a thought leader, and maintaining that profile, requires financial success. Only by staying abreast of the economic returns from a thought leadership initiative and understanding how to better the endeavor will your firm learn how to derive optimal benefits from becoming a thought leader.

In many ways, monetization drives how to best become and stay a thought leader. Specifically, monetization guides strategy. For example, it helps clarify and refine goals. It also is instrumental in garnering managing partner support and hence requisite resources.

Not surprisingly, we've found that as thought leadership initiatives result in new and expanded client engagements that translate into significant revenues for the firm, the support for thought leadership initiatives seriously increases. Hence, to refine and improve a firm's thought leadership initiatives as well as build internal commitment, it's important to be able to prove that for your firm, being a thought leader is an extraordinarily effective and powerful approach to business development.

FOOD FOR THOUGHT

Forbes is about capitalism. Forbes is about success. Forbes is about thought leadership.

Forbes Insights brings many of the outstanding talents housed at Forbes and its affiliated companies to help professional services firms and other organizations become thought leaders as well as celebrity thought leaders. Forbes Insights is about significantly facilitating business development by assisting firms through the thought leadership process.

As we noted in *Chapter 6: The Thought Leadership Process*, there isn't any magic in what we do. While we are quite adept, that doesn't mean we're unique. Nor does it mean that a professional services firm cannot become a thought leader by exclusively employing internal resources.

What we never lose sight of, though it's sometimes invisible to more than a few managing partners, is the need to make thought leadership pay off—and pay off exceptionally well. We're often engaged for that purpose, and we have to regularly refocus the managing partners on the goals of their thought leadership initiative—the financial end goal, the strategic goals and the intermediary goals.

What you must never do is lose your bearings. Becoming a thought leader is absolutely about better positioning yourselves as the go-to professionals for a sleeve of services— "brains." In every meeting, in every discussion, in every assignment, you and the other managing partners at your firm must always understand how becoming a thought leader is going to help swell the firm's as well as the individual partners' bank accounts.

INTERLUDE: CAPTAIN OF THE TEAM

RICK FLYNN, MANAGING PARTNER, ROTHSTEIN KASS

Rick Flynn is one of the most successful and sought-after experts on running a Family Office practice—a practice he started at accounting firm Rothstein Kass in 2002. His position as a profitable thought leader came later in life, and his path is one full of shining examples of our precepts in action of the steps you, too, can take to earn a similar role for in your business.

While experiencing what many would consider the pinnacle of business success fairly early in his career as an entrepreneur, he had not yet found what he refers to as his "calling in life" until the last several years with Rothstein Kass. Similar to many profitable thought leaders, Rick became both more successful and happy in life by combining his life-long passions and natural gifts with a disciplined process through which he achieved his solid thought leadership position in the Family Office universe.

Rick has been a leader since his childhood little league days on Long Island. With the same hard work, dedication, desire to succeed and love of team camaraderie, he demonstrated then, and he continues to expand and improve his skills, test himself among the best competition, and be the good teammate everyone can count on. Still looking the part of an athlete, Rick (and the team he assembled at Rothstein Kass) makes his living providing a host of accounting services, a broad range of sophisticated tax advice, legal insights and "life management" services to the ultra high net worth families Rothstein Kass serves within their Family Office Practice.

Though successful by most measurements, Rick felt he was the proverbial "jack of all trades and a master of none." He didn't feel 100% comfortable in his own skin in what he was meant to do in life. So he developed a plan: make the Rothstein Kass' Family Office practice at least as successful as its hedge fund practice, which is recognized around the world as a leader in this field, allowing Rothstein Kass to compete and win business against the much larger big four accounting firms.

Every year Rick writes down his personal and professional development goals and his primary goal was to create a path toward profitable thought leadership for his practice and for his team at Rothstein Kass. To facilitate these goals, he found an experienced coach in Russ Prince. With Russ's guidance, and Rick perseverance and willingness to expand his skill sets, Rick began to create content based on his goals and expertise. This entailed, in part, in developing intellectual capital addressing the issues and concerns of the high net worth clients as well as the best practices in the Family Office universe. The intellectual capital would then be turned into products and distributed and highlighted in relevant trade journals and targeted research-based industry reports. He recalls being fearful at first as he forced himself to move outside of his comfort zone, not being an experienced public speaker and never having written for a wide audience.

Today, he is the co-author of two books (*Fame & Fortune* and *The Family Office*) and is an internationally sought-after expert on the complex business of building a successful Family Office practice as well as the intricacies of working with high net worth clients as well as the super-rich. More importantly, he and his team at Rothstein Kass have monetized his well-earned thought leadership status in ways that exceeded his own ambitious goals. Since starting down this business a little more than 5 years ago, Rick's personal book of business—defined as annual recurring revenue—has grown more than 1,500%. Meanwhile, the growth trajectory for the Rothstein Kass Family Office practice just continues to escalate. Along the way, Rick's "jack of all trades" mentality and skills ironically now form the very basis of his success with clients. He now enjoys being a problem solver as well as the camaraderie and relationship building that comes from managing his clients' affairs.

CODA: THE FUTURE OF PROFITABLE BRILLIANCE

When a professional services firm is a thought leader, and even more so when it's a celebrity thought leader, it has distinct and powerful business development advantages over its competitors. These advantages are readily becoming clear—presuming they're not already apparent—to the overwhelming majority of managing partners at professional services firms. There's absolutely no question about the multiple and meaningful payback of being profitably brilliant.

That being the case, thought leadership is evolving in a host of ways. Looking forward, for example, we see four interconnected trends:

- Everyone into the pool.
- The decisive battlefield.
- Raising the bar.
- Cooperating to excel.

Let's take a closer look at each of these trends.

EVERYONE INTO THE POOL

As we just noted, for a professional services firm, the power of being a thought leader is tremendous. Within the last half dozen or so years, the number of professional services firms intent on becoming thought leaders has exploded. A few key factors are driving the very strong appeal; we addressed some of them in *Chapter 4: The Case for Thought Leadership*. The most important factor, we would argue, is the ability for professional services firms to build their businesses in hypercompetitive environments with often persnickety clients.

Business Implication: Because of the business-building power that accrues to thought leaders, a growing number of managing partners are going to increasingly take actions so that their firms are thought leaders. While the market for professional services firms wanting to be thought leaders is quickly becoming saturated, the market for stellar thought leadership is not.

THE DECISIVE BATTLEFIELD

As professional services are almost completely fungible and often impossible for prospects, referral sources and even clients to evaluate, the competition for thought leadership status increasingly is becoming the cornerstone of success for many professional services firms. What's painfully clear is that almost any professional services firm can be profitably brilliant—regardless of its talents. The very same thought leadership process that can transform a Hidden Talent into a Talented Expert can transform an Incompetent into an Incompetent Expert. The quality of the thought leadership initiative can readily overshadow the quality of the firm's capabilities.

Business Implication: There will be an increasing bifurcation of professional services firms, between the relative few that are thought leaders and the majority that are not. Considering that all professional services firms are fungible—which in no way disclaims the fact that some firms are objectively better than others—being a thought leader will increasingly make the essential difference to a firm's financial success.

RAISING THE BAR

As more and more professional services firms look to become thought leaders, the costs are only going to rise. To develop and distribute high-quality thought leadership products in a crowded field, where all kinds of information bombards the target audiences, requires the professional services firm's deliverables to stand apart. In this ultra-competitive environment, the thought leadership products can't just stand out a little—they have to enable the professional services firm to pull five or six lengths away from its many competitors.

Business Implication: With becoming a thought leader more and more looking like the pot of gold at the end of the rainbow, managing partners are going to have to seriously commit to the endeavor, or they should avoid it altogether. With competition among professional services firms escalating, the absolute quality of a firm's thought leadership products will have to continually reach greater heights to have a positive impact on the firm's finances.

COOPERATING TO EXCEL

The need to develop and distribute exceptional thought leadership products, coupled with the various expenses to produce such high-caliber material, means we'll see more and more professional services firms teaming up. For a great many professional services firms, it can be a daunting task to commit the time and energy as well as bring together all the needed resources. The ability to craft the initiative or campaign that will make your firm a thought leader, let alone a celebrity thought leader, may also be something that's not within your firm's area of expertise, consequently requiring cooperation with other firms or organizations.

Business Implication: The need to produce outstanding thought leadership products is intensifying, which is driving up all the costs. To address the burgeoning cost structure as well as deftly expand distribution channels, many professional services firms are well served by teaming up.

A FINAL BUSINESS IMPLICATION

What's the future of profitable brilliance?

As the pop band Timbuk 3 put it: "The future's so bright, I gotta wear shades." Being a thought leader, let alone a celebrity thought leader, is undeniably exceedingly advantageous for any professional services firm, and that is why the appeal of this marketing approach is only going to skyrocket.

Now, what are YOU going to do?

APPENDICES

APPENDIX A:
MONEY RULES

It's fair to say that most people want to be wealthy. Just consider the throngs who buy lottery tickets—and even more of them do so when the jackpots get really large. The desire for wealth—especially extreme wealth—is pervasive in our society. We're not discounting other needs and wants, but being rich tends to be right up at the top of the preferential hierarchy for a great many people. What's even more revealing is that for an awful lot of people, while rich is certainly good, very rich is even better.

Over the last few decades, we've been able to empirically and experientially identify the most likely ways to become seriously wealthy. While we've evaluated the mechanisms for significant wealth creation at various levels of affluence, the work we've done with the self-made super-rich—individuals who've created personal fortunes of US$500 million or greater—is the most illuminating. Here we're seeing the means to creating extreme wealth without the patina of propriety.

Based primarily on ethnological investigations, coupled with select supporting quantitative research, we've been able to ascertain and conceptualize the mindset and behaviors that enable the self-made super-rich to create their immense fortunes. We refer to these ways of thinking and actions as the Money Rules. While we see personal variations in the level of intensity when it comes to adopting the Money Rules, there's no question that in the right minds and hands, they provide a powerful means to generating Croesus-level wealth.

There are a number of Money Rules. A person achieves optimal results by using the rules in concert. Implementing just one of them, while likely to better a person's economic station, is highly beneficial but nonetheless will have a limited effect. When the Money Rules are skillfully applied in a holistic and integrated manner, while tightly customized to an individual's idiosyncratic situation, it's possible to achieve an exponential boost in net worth. Then, if a person truly, wholeheartedly and intensely embraces the Money Rules, using them as a guide for all aspects of his or her business and much of his or her personal life, it's very possible to amass a spectacularly colossal fortune.

AN OVERVIEW OF THE MONEY RULES

What follows are a number of the critical Money Rules that can be core to your becoming fabulously wealthy:

1. Commit to extreme wealth.
2. Engage in enlightened self-interest.
3. Put yourself in the line of money.
4. Pay everyone involved.
5. Connect for profit and results.
6. Use failure to improve and refocus.
7. Stay highly centered.

While, as noted, the Money Rules work best in concert, for purposes of simplicity and brevity, let's consider these "rules of conduct" individually.

1. Commit to extreme wealth. Truth be told, many people would like to be rich but haven't committed the time or effort necessary to get there. Doing so can often mean being faced with choices that help you reach your goal of being wealthy at the expense of something else that may be important to you. Following this rule means having a clear sense that money is one of your objectives, if not your most critical objective, and consciously prioritizing activities with the highest potential return and assigning a lower priority to almost everything else in your life.

2. Engage in enlightened self-interest. Today's society praises caring, compromise and collaboration as a way to find the common ground where people (or institutions) with different aims and vantage points can realize enough of their goals to be satisfied. While that approach is comfortable, especially for those who detest confrontation, it gains the abhorrence of most ambitious and successful people. The wealthiest among us are focused on reaching their milestones and financial end goals, and never waver or allow themselves to be derailed by the chance for group happiness or pleas for fairness and justice.

3. Put yourself in the line of money. Simply put, some endeavors are more fruitful and rewarding than others. Since most skills are portable, it only makes sense that the self-made super-rich apply theirs in the situations that offer the highest paybacks. Following this rule means pursuing the fields and initiatives that have the utmost potential for outsize returns, now and in the future. As we noted (see *Chapter 3: What Is a Thought Leader?*), when your professional services firm becomes a thought leader, that astutely places the firm, your partners and you in the line of money.

4. Pay everyone involved. The exceedingly wealthy assume that everyone has a degree of self-interest that can be used to their advantage, and they target that nature in others when building a team around themselves. They never assume that people are willing to work for satisfaction or fulfillment, and therefore they reward handsomely—with cash, equity or some other form of currency—in an effort to cultivate the loyalty and specific behaviors in their colleagues that can help them advance toward their personal milestones and financial goals. As we first noted in *Chapter 4: The Case for Thought Leadership*, thought leadership products can be a powerful way to pay referral sources.

5. *Connect for profit and results*. Highly successful people think about networking as a means to an end—finding the person, the information or the tools that get them one step closer to their personal and professional objectives. Following this rule means maintaining a small but deep network of relationships that lead not to friendship but to power and influence. This form of nodal networking maximizes the time and effort spent on realizing profit and identifying those things that can further enhance your profit (see *Appendix C: Elite Professional Networks*).

6. *Use failure to improve and refocus*. Failure is inevitable, so most of the self-made super-rich don't worry about avoiding it. Instead, they focus on learning from each experience and using the lessons to gain an advantage the next time around. Rather than obsessing about lost opportunities and getting discouraged, you should study your failures and do all you can to prevent repeating missteps. By autopsying our failures and learning well from them, we exponentially improved our ability to craft and manage thought leadership initiatives and campaigns (see *Chapter 9: Monetizing*).

7. *Stay highly centered*. The wealthiest among us know there are just a few things they do truly well, so they focus on what they want to achieve and what role those primary skills play in generating wealth. Being highly centered means sticking to your plan and not getting distracted by other opportunities or events that call for new and different skill sets. The self-made super-rich are exceptionally capable of focusing themselves and delegating to others in a way that leaves little room for derailment or doubt.

A good way to understand the power and purpose of these rules is to compare them to the typical approach of a seriously successful business professional or middle-class millionaire, someone with emerging wealth but clearly not one of the super-rich (see Exhibit A.1). As you'll see, the behaviors considered acceptable in most social or professional environments are designed to promote harmony and mutually beneficial but often quasi-successful outcomes, rather than substantial wealth or clear winners. The comparison is generalized to show the differences.

EXHIBIT A.1: DIFFERENT TAKES

Money Rules	Middle-Class Millionaire	Super-Rich
1. Commit to extreme wealth	Look for work-life balance, where money is one piece of this equation	Creating wealth in the powerful driving motivation and objective
2. Engage in enlightened self-interest	Look to make everyone "happy" or get a fair deal	Make sure that in every meaningful situation they are winners–strategically and/or financially
3. Put yourself in the line of money	Believe in doing what they love– the money will follow	Pursue only those activities that have, or are perceived to have, significant probabilities of generating radically above-average financial returns
4. Pay everyone involved	Create rapport and look to help others	Ensure that each party is duly compensated
5. Connect for profit and results	Network with a lot of people	Build strong relationships with a few strategically valuable people
6. Use failure to improve and refocus	Failure proves to be a major obstacle	Failure is a learning experience and a motivator
7. Stay highly centered	Concentrate on overcoming weaknesses	Concentrate on a very few especially strong appropriate strengths and delegate everything else

FOR YOUR CONSIDERATION

Most people can likely capitalize on the Money Rules in two ways. One way is very direct: You can make them central to the way you approach your own career and personal wealth-building activities. We refer to this approach as the individual application of the Money Rules.

You can, however, take the Money Rules to heart for yourself and ardently into the corporate environment. This is when you dexterously and shrewdly adopt the Money Rules within the operational parameters of your professional services firm. To understand and see the results of such a strategy, go through the following exercise:

Step 1: For each of the Money Rules, identify how it can be applied within your professional services firm. The applications should deal with both the business functioning within the firm and the firm's dealing with prospects, clients, referral sources, vendors, joint-venture partners, competitors and the like.

Step 2: Specify the projected outcomes of adopting the Money Rules with respect to each possible application. As you'll likely come up with a number of possible outcomes, focus on the three you believe have the highest probability of occurring.

Step 3: For each of the outcomes, spell out the likely consequences—good and bad—for your firm and yourself. You have to pay attention to the downside as well as the upside. You would be best served if you can come up with some financials to go along with the outcomes.

Step 4: Based on your analysis, where would the applications of the Money Rules make the most sense? You cannot tackle every possibility. You'll need to triage the opportunities with the aim of maximizing your results.

While we started this section by parceling the application of the Money Rules between the individual and the corporate entity, it's really an artificial distinction. The distinction between individual and corporation is only applicable to the likes of executives with little or no control over the direction of the firm that employs them. It's important to note that when it comes to the self-made super-rich, for a great many of them, there is often no genuine division between themselves and their holdings.

Presumably, you're in a position at your professional services firm where you can determine or influence the actions, and therefore the future, of the firm. If this is indeed the case, then by embracing and implementing the Money Rules, you're driving your firm to tremendously greater financial achievements. As a product of your firm's greater and greater success, coupled with your more personal adoption of the Money Rules, you're in the process of potentially creating your very own Brobdingnagian fortune.

APPENDIX B:
CREATING STRATEGIC PARTNERSHIPS WITH REFERRAL SOURCES

For professional services firms, very often referral sources are essential to building a high-quality clientele. A great many professional services firms garner their best new clients from other professionals. Consequently, many firms and the professionals therein are actively looking to develop meaningful relationships with referral sources. However, relatively few firms are doing an especially good job at developing these often-necessary meaningful relationships. Part of the problem is a misunderstanding concerning what really constitutes a meaningful relationship.

Many professional services firms are highly motivated to create strategic alliances with referral sources. What they really need to do is create relationships that result in a pipeline of new clients—strategic partnerships (see Exhibit B.1).

With strategic alliances, your firm will usually get some client referrals. However, these introductions are generally sporadic at best. By contrast, in a strategic partnership, the referral sources will be providing your firm with a consistent stream of clients needing your firm's expertise and are motivated to talk with your partners—and only with your partners.

Professional services firms who have strategic alliances are often one of a number of similar firms doing business with a referral source. In a strategic partnership, your firm is the exclusive (or the highly preferred) expert, and will receive the bulk, if not all, of the referrals.

As a strategic partner, the referral source is actively looking to direct clients to your firm. The same cannot be said for strategic alliances.

EXHIBIT B.1: COMPARISON OF STRATEGIC ALLIANCES AND STRATEGIC PARTNERSHIPS

Strategic Alliances	*Strategic Partnerships*
Periodically a client will be referred to your firm	On a regular basis, clients are referred to your firm
Your firm is one of a number of similar firms to whom referrals are made for a specific expertise	Your firm is the only or the primary professional services firm to whom referrals are made for a specific expertise
The referral source is not particularly looking to make an introduction	The referral source is actively looking to make an introduction

MAKING RAIN

What's evident is that most professional services firms are mistakenly striving to establish strategic alliances as opposed to strategic partnerships. They regularly miss the mark badly with this approach, because it's usually all about them. The professionals at the firm tend to focus the discussions with potential referral sources on their own abilities and competencies, ending with how good they are. In contrast, professionals need to profile prospective referral sources and, if it makes sense to pursue the relationship, provide economic glue to cement the strategic partnership (see Exhibit B.2).

EXHIBIT B.2: MAKING RAIN

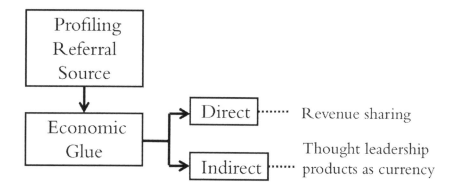

Professionals shouldn't be focusing the conversation with potential referral sources on themselves and their firms. This is super-
fluous, especially if your firm has a powerful dual-impact brand
(see *Chapter 5: Fame, Then Fortunes*). The dual-impact brand will
provide referral sources with a positive image that incorporates
the expertise your firm can deliver. Instead of pontificating, professionals need to profile potential referral sources. In profiling
those sources, we recommend that you employ a graphic analytic structure (see Exhibit B.3). The following are the components of the profile:

- *Referral source.* Identify the facts that will form the basis of
  this firm's profile, such as the details of the key professionals, including relevant demographics.
- *Firm goals and objectives.* Understand what the referral
  source wants to accomplish professionally. What are
  its biggest obstacles and what have been its greatest
  successes?
- *Current clientele.* Whom does the referral source currently
  work with? How many of these clients fit the criteria your
  firm is interested in?

- *Marketing strategy.* How is the referral source sourcing clients? What has the referral source tried recently to bring in clients? How has it worked out and why?
- *Practice dynamics.* How does the business of the referral source operate? What is the compensation structure at the referral source?
- *Expertise.* What are the referral source's areas of competency? Are there any fields of specialization in which it is notably proficient?
- *Rainmakers.* Who are the key business development professionals at the referral source? Why are they there?

EXHIBIT B.3: PROFILING REFERRAL SOURCES

Probably the biggest obstacle to creating strategic partnerships is that professionals are not inclined and/or proficient at effectively profiling referral sources. Having extensively trained many different types of professionals in how to develop strategic partnerships, we constantly find that they fall back on the fact that they perceive themselves as authorities and believe that if they explain this ardently to a potential referral source, that referral source will see the logic of sending over clients. To establish strategic partnerships, it's imperative that the professionals at your firm be adept at profiling potential and current referral sources.

After profiling a referral source and deciding that this organization is able and potentially willing to direct clients your way, your firm must motivate the principals at the organization to do so. We refer to this as the economic glue. There are two ways you can do this—direct and indirect financial incentives. Direct financial incentives include revenue sharing and reciprocal referrals.

Revenue sharing is the optimal form of economic glue. However, it's not viable in a great many situations. At the same time, we're not in favor of trading clients. In fact, the essence of this approach is about not referring your clients while still getting client referrals. While the concept of reciprocal referrals sounds good and fair, it usually proves untenable.

Indirect financial incentives are ways for you to help the referral source become more successful. You can effectively "pay" referral sources with high-caliber thought leadership products. Your ability to deliver business-based solutions to referral sources, for example, which in turn enables them to be more profitable, can act as economic superglue, motivating them to refer their best clients to you.

ELITE PROFESSIONAL NETWORKS

If a core objective for your professional services firm is to work with a steady stream of high-caliber clients, sourcing them through referral sources is likely paramount. In the previous appendix, we addressed the rudimentary aspects of the strategic partnering process. Thought leadership can be integral in motivating referral sources to utilize your firm's expertise on behalf of their clients. The optimal result of strategic partnering—where your firm is taking the process as far as it can go—is the establishment of an elite professional network.

Elite professional networks are, by design, primarily composed of some combination of non-overlapping professional services firms delivering complementary and often supportive expertise. The unquestioned objective for the members of an elite professional network is to strategically and tactically cooperate to source and share exceptional clients.

There are times when elite professional networks are arrangements between firms. At other times—and this is more often the case—the networks are established among a handful of professionals from various firms.

ROLES WITHIN AN ELITE PROFESSIONAL NETWORK
All the professionals directly involved in the network tend to have multiple roles. Basically, there are four distinct, but interrelated, roles within every elite professional network:
- Rainmakers.
- Client facilitators.

- Meta-facilitators.
- Technical specialists.

Let's now consider each of these roles.

Rainmakers. They're the heart of any elite professional network, and central to its effectiveness. Rainmakers are the members who bring in outstanding clients to their own firm as well as the other firms composing the network. While any member of the network can be, and is encouraged to be, a rainmaker, the same professionals tend to bring in most of the clients.

The iconic positioning that rainmakers derive from developing and distributing high-caliber thought leadership products often proves essential in enabling them to distinguish themselves among prospects, clients and referral sources. This, in turn, allows them to regularly bring clients to other members of their elite professional network.

Client facilitators. The very nature of the elite professional network is predicated on sharing clients with other members of the network. It's important to note that the sharing among members of the network must be highly proactive. This also means that the members work to keep nonmembers away. The responsibility for making this happen falls to the client facilitator.

The client facilitator is usually the lead professional working with any particular client. There are times when the client facilitator is the rainmaker. However, this is not always the case. When the core expertise desired by the client is the province of a different professional services firm within the network than the rainmaker's, it's very likely that a professional from that other firm becomes the client facilitator.

The critical function of the client facilitator is to, where and when appropriate, make sure the other members of the elite professional network are brought in. To be able to effectively bring in those other members, the client facilitator must have a broad and in-depth understanding of the capabilities of the Savants at the other firms.

Meta-facilitators. These professionals generally get involved in mediating differences among the handful of members, thereby keeping everyone aligned. To the extent that the network members pool resources, the meta-facilitators are often the ones responsible for managing those projects. They have to work with all the members to ensure that no one feels slighted as they contribute time, energy and monies.

In some elite professional networks, money moves internally. Fees, for example, are shared among some—rarely all—of the members. The meta-facilitator is typically involved to ensure all parties are paid without complications. Hence, he or she has to be aware of the pricing for all the services the elite professional network is providing to each client.

Technical specialists. Each professional services firm and each representative professional who is part of the network is a technical specialist. This means each member brings a certain top-of-the-line expertise to each client engagement. Rarely are competing technical specialists in the same network.

To be accepted into the network, the other professional services firms, as well as the individual professionals from those firms, must conclude that the technical capabilities a particular firm, as well as its partners, brings to the table are unquestionably top-flight. Each member of the network has to have total confidence that the other professionals will be able to do their job expertly as well as be truly client-centered. If any one of the professionals in the network falters, it reflects badly on the rest of the members and will likely result in the client disengaging at some level.

THE FUTURE OF ELITE PROFESSIONAL NETWORKS

We currently know of a fair number of elite professional networks, dispersed throughout the world. We've even done some consulting for a few of them, which tends to entail developing high-caliber dual-impact brands and accompanying thought leadership products, and improving the effectiveness of the network and the businesses of members firms.

While the business model of elite professional networks is extraordinarily profitable, it's highly unlikely that this business model will become in any way normative. Although it's certainly possible, if not advisable, for high-quality professional services firms to form these networks, a lot has to do with chemistry among the managing partners as well as among the professionals within the firms.

For the overwhelming majority of adept professional services firms, the best practices embraced by elite professional networks can be very constructive. For example, the ability to ensure achievement of the total return on each high-caliber client would certainly benefit every professional involved. By adopting some of the strategies and tactics that make these networks so effective and profitable, professional services firms can certainly improve their own chances of business success.

ABOUT FORBES INSIGHTS

Forbes Insights is the strategic research practice of Forbes Media, publisher of Forbes magazine and Forbes.com. Taking advantage of a proprietary database of senior-level executives in the Forbes community, Forbes Insights' research covers a wide range of vital business issues including: talent management; marketing; financial benchmarking; risk and regulation; small/mid-size business; economic and industry outlooks and innovation.

ABOUT THE AUTHORS

Russ Alan Prince is president of Prince & Associates, Inc. He consults with a select and oft times esoteric clientele on dramatically growing their businesses. His track record of success is predicated on helping them become high-caliber industry thought leaders coupled with an intense focus on personal wealth creation.

Bruce H. Rogers is the Chief Insights Officer for Forbes Media responsible for managing Forbes' Insights thought leadership research division, as well as the Forbes CMO Practice. His previous book, *In the Line of Money: Branding Yourself Strategically to the Financial Elite*, co-authored by Russ Alan Prince, is available on Amazon.

For more insights on thought leadership, go to: http://blogs.forbes.com/russprince/

Made in the USA
Lexington, KY
29 May 2013